SELECTE

Wole Soyinka was born in Niger... Government College, Ibadan and t...   ....u s Leeds University, and worked in British theatre before returning to Nigeria in 1960. His earlier prose works include *The Interpreters*, which was awarded the Jock Campbell Prize for Commonwealth Literature. Wole Soyinka received a New Statesman John Whiting Award for 1966–7 and was Overseas Fellow at Churchill College, Cambridge in 1973–4, where he wrote the widely acclaimed *Death and the King's Horseman*. He has been awarded the George Benson Medal of the Royal Society for Literature and the UNESCO Medal for the Arts. In 1986 he became the first African writer to win the Nobel Prize for Literature. Forced into exile in 1994 by military dictatorship, he returned home four years later and now divides his time between Nigeria and overseas universities.

by the same author

POETRY
Idanre and Other Poems
Ogun Abibiman
Mandela's Earth
A Shuttle in the Crypt

PLAYS
The Bacchae of Euripides
The Beatification of Area Boy
Camwood on the Leaves
A Dance of the Forests
Death and the King's Horseman
From Zia, With Love
The Jero Plays
Kongi's Harvest
The Lion and the Jewel
Madmen and Specialists
Opera Wonyosi
A Play of Giants
Requiem for a Futurologist
The Road
A Scourge of Hyacinths
The Strong Breed
The Swamp Dwellers

FICTION
The Interpreters
Season of Anomy

MEMOIRS
Aké, The Years of Childhood
Ibadan, The Penkelemes Years
Ìsarà, A Voyage Around Essay
The Man Died (Prison Notes)

ESSAYS ON ART AND CULTURE
Art, Dialogue and Outrage
Myth; Literature and the African World

WOLE SOYINKA

—

SELECTED POEMS

Idanre
A Shuttle in the Crypt
Mandela's Earth

Methuen

Methuen

3 5 7 9 10 8 6 4 2

Idanre first published in 1967
by Methuen & Co Ltd
A Shuttle in the Crypt first published in 1972
by Rex Collings Ltd and Eyre Methuen & Co Ltd
Mandela's Earth first published in 1989
by André Deutsch Limited

This collection first published in Great Britain in 2001by
Methuen Publishing Limited
11-12 Buckingham Gate,
London SW1E 6LB

Copyright © 1967, 1972, 1989 Wole Soyinka

Methuen Publishing Ltd Reg. No. 3543167

A CIP catalogue record for this book is available from the British Library

ISBN 0 413 76460 5

Typeset by Deltatype Ltd, Birkenhead, Merseyside

Printed and bound in Great Britain
by Cox & Wyman Ltd, Reading, Berkshire

CONTENTS

Idanre

Of the Road

Lone Figure

Of Birth and Death

For Women

Grey Seasons

October '66

Idanre

———

A Shuttle in the Crypt

Prisonnettes

Poems of Bread and Earth

Epilogue

———

Mandela's Earth

Deluge and After

U.S.A.

Ile-Ife

Idanre

—

Of the Road

DAWN

Breaking earth upon
A spring-haired elbow, lone
A palm beyond head-grains, spikes
A guard of prim fronds, piercing
High hairs of the wind

As one who bore the pollen highest

Blood-drops in the air, above
The even belt of tassels, above
Coarse leaf teasing on the waist, steals
The lone intruder, tearing wide

The chaste hide of the sky

O celebration of the rites of dawn
Night-spread in tatters and a god
Received, aflame with kernels.

DEATH IN THE DAWN

*Driving to Lagos one morning a white cockerel flew out of the dusk
and smashed itself against my windscreen. A mile further I came
across a motor accident and a freshly dead man in the smash.*

Traveller, you must set out
At dawn. And wipe your feet upon
The dog-nose wetness of earth.

Let sunrise quench your lamps, and watch
Faint brush pricklings in the sky light
Cottoned feet to break the early earthworm
On the hoe. Now shadows stretch with sap
Not twilight's death and sad prostration.

This soft kindling, soft receding breeds
Racing joys and apprehensions for
A naked day. Burdened hulks retract,
Stoop to the mist in faceless throng
To wake the silent markets – swift, mute
Processions on grey byways. . . .

On this
Counterpane, it was –
Sudden winter at the death
Of dawn's lone trumpeter, cascades
Of white feather-flakes, but it proved
A futile rite. Propitiation sped
Grimly on, before.

The right foot for joy, the left, dread
And the mother prayed, Child
May you never walk
When the road waits, famished.

Traveller you must set forth
At dawn
I promise marvels of the holy hour
Presages as the white cock's flapped
Perverse impalement – as who would dare
The wrathful wings of man's Progression. . . .

But such another Wraith! Brother,
Silenced in the startled hug of
Your invention – is this mocked grimace
This closed contortion – I?

AROUND US, DAWNING

Jet flight

This beast was fashioned well; it prowls
The rare selective heights
And spurns companionship with bird

Wings are tipped in sulphurs
Scouring grey recesses of the void
To a linear flare of dawns

Red haloes through the ports wreathe us
Passive martyrs, bound to a will of rotors

Yielding ours,
To the alien mote
The hidden ache ... when
Death makes a swift descent

The mountains range in spire on spire
Lances at the bold carbuncle
On the still night air. I am light honed

To a still point in the incandescent
Onrush, a fine ash in the beast's sudden
Dessication when the sun explodes.

LUO PLAINS

Kenya

Plague
Of comet tails, of bled horizons
Where egrets hone a sky-lane for
Worlds to turn on pennants

Lakemists
On her shadeless dugs, parched
At waterhole. Veils. Molten silver
Down cloudflues of alchemist sun . . .
A lake's grey salve at dawn?

That dawn
Her eyes were tipped with sunset spears
Seasons' quills upon her parchment, yet
The hidden lake of her

Forgives!

For she has milked a cycle of
Red sunset spears, sucked reeds of poison
To a cowherd's flute. The plains
Are swift again on migrant wings
And the cactus
Flowers the eagle sentinel.

IN MEMORY OF SEGUN AWOLOWO

For him who was
Lifted on tar sprays
And gravel rains

In metallic timbres
Harder than milestone heart

For him who was.

The road, the aged road
Retched on this fresh plunder
Of my youth

An error of the sun
A mirage upon earth's
Apostate face

For him who fell among reapers
Who forestall the harvest

And drove
The last flint deepest
In the heart of patience

Death the scrap-iron dealer
Breeds a glut on trade. The fault
Is His of seven paths whose whim
Gave Death his agency

In sounds as of the river's
Failing pulse, of shifting earth
They make complaint

Grey presences of head and hands
Who wander still
Adrift from understanding.

Lone Figure

THE DREAMER

Higher than trees a cryptic crown
Lord of the rebel three
Thorns lay on a sleep of down
And myrrh; a mesh
Of nails, of flesh
And words that flowered free

A cleft between the birches
Next year is reaping time
The fruit will fall to searchers
Cleansed of mould
Chronicles of gold
Mourn a fruit in prime.

The burden bowed the boughs to earth
A girdle for the see
And bitter pods gave voices birth
A ring of stones
And throes and thrones
And incense on the sea.

THE HUNCHBACK OF DUGBE

I wondered always where
He walked at night, or lay
Where earth might seem
Suddenly in labour when he sighed.

By day, stooped at public drains
Intense at bath or washing cotton holes,
An ant's blown load upon
A child's entangled scrawl

The calmest nudist
Of the roadside lunatics.

The devil came one sane night
On parole from hell, lace curtains
Sieved light dancing pebbles
On his vast creation egg

His cement mixer borne
On crossed cassava sticks.

Not in disdain, but in truth immune
From song or terror, taxi turns
And sale fuss of the mad, beyond
Ugliness or beauty, whom thought-sealing

Solemnly transfigures – the world
Spins on his spine, in still illusion.

But the bell-tower of his thin
Buttocks rings pure tones on Dugbe
A horse penis loin to crooked knees
Side-slapping on his thighs

At night he prowls, a cask
Of silence; on his lone matrix
Pigeon eggs of light dance in and out
Of dark, and he walks in motley.

THE LAST LAMP

A pale
Incision in the skin of night
It dwindled downhill, weaker bled
From pole to passage, dye
And shroud

Her shadow
Now indrawn from dances
On the silent eaves
Gathers close about her –
A lying depth

Oil is a kindly lamp
To generations' patient stoop
In crooked doorways, to a market's
Final breath

Of patience, peace denied . . .
She was a vespers' valediction, lit
Within deserted ribs.

EASTER

This slow day dies, a wordless wilt
Shades of silence reaping
Soft frangipanes

Pollen's wings are thorned; bosoms
Too welcoming fold later chills
Take death to innocents

Kinder these hard mangoes, greendrops
At the ear of god-apparent, coquettes
To the future decadence.

Do we not truly fear to bleed? We hunt
Pale tissues of the palm, fingers groping
Ever cautious on the crown.

These pink frangipanes of Easter crop
Eager to the wind; by repetition weak
And rain's in-breeding,

One bough to slake the millions? Decay
Caulks earth's centre; spurned we pluck
Bleached petals for the dreamer's lair.

Borne passive on this gift, wound-splashes
From wind scavenger, sap fragrance for
A heady brew, I rode my winged ass and raged –

As children wove frond yellow from the palm
Plucked at the core, within the spadix heart.

Of Birth and Death

KOKO OLORO

From a children's propitiation chant

Dolorous knot
Plead for me
Farm or hill
Plead for me
Stream and wind
Take my voice
Home or road
Plead for me
On this shoot, I
Bind your leaves
Stalk and bud
Berries three
On the threshold
Cast my voice
Knot of bitters
Plead for me.

DEDICATION

For Moremi, 1963

Earth will not share the rafter's envy: dung floors
Break, not the gecko's slight skin, but its fall
Taste this soil for death and plumb her deep for life

As this yam, wholly earthed, yet a living tuber
To the warmth of waters, earthed as springs
As roots of baobab, as the hearth.

The air will not deny you. Like a top
Spin you on the navel of the storm, for the hoe
That roots the forests ploughs a path for squirrels.

Be ageless as dark peat, but only that rain's
Fingers, not the feet of men may wash you over.
Long wear the sun's shadow; run naked to the night.

Peppers green and red – child – your tongue arch
To scorpion tail, spit straight return to danger's threats
Yet coo with the brown pigeon, tendril dew between your
        lips.

Shield you like the flesh of palms, skyward held
Cuspids in thorn nesting, insealed as the heart of kernel –
A woman's flesh is oil – child, palm oil on your tongue

Is suppleness to life, and wine of this gourd
From self-same timeless run of runnels as refill
Your podlings, child, weaned from yours we embrace

Earth's honeyed milk, wine of the only rib.
Now roll your tongue in honey till your cheeks are
Swarming honeycombs – your world needs sweetening,
    child.

Camwood round the heart, chalk for flight
Of blemish – see? it dawns! – antimony beneath
Armpits like a goddess, and leave this taste

Long on your lips, of salt, that you may seek
None from tears. This, rain-water, is the gift
Of gods – drink of its purity, bear fruits in season.

Fruits then to your lips: haste to repay
The debt of birth. Yield man-tides like the sea
And ebbing, leave a meaning on the fossilled sands.

A CRY IN THE NIGHT

Burial of a still-born

As who would break
Earth, grief
In savage pounding, moulds
Her forehead where she kneels.

No stars caress her keening
The sky recedes from pain

Nor will this night dark
Shield her. Defiance falls back
Barren, heaven may not contest
Scars, shower ancient scales
To prove her torment shared.

Such tender stalk is earthed
In haste. A stricken snake, she drags
Across the gulf, re-enters to the retch
Of grieving wombs. Night harshly folds her
Broken as her afterbirth.

A FIRST DEATHDAY

We triumphed then upon the wails of birth
And felt no fears. By mute assertion
Of the later year, she marked *her* victory
Grief has long receded, yet the wonder
Stays.

Truly, it was a deed of grace, this death
At the first teething, contrary
Precision of her first birthday, almost
On the hour.

Knowledge as this in growth's diffusion
Thins, till shrouds are torn from swaddlings.
She was not one more veil, dark across
The Secret; Folasade ran bridal to the Spouse
Wise to fore-planning – bear witness, Time
To my young will, in this last breath
Of mockery.

FOR THE PIPER DAUGHTERS (1960)

Seeking – as who has not? – beauty
Lodged in concaves of the yielded;
Conniving lies with self-encrimsoned mists,
Your laugh
       Meant,
Your warmth,
       Given,
And innocence
       Lightly
As your next footfall – unpractised,
Left after right – this, your revelation
Unmasks past seemings.

I would not have you cruel, nor change
Your largesse for the slits
In hoarded goodness – yet
To the date
       A stone
The linnet
       Height
Pearls
       Depth and the clam;
The rose, you know, is thorned. And if
The cozening priest would slay you, panting
How your cheeks are rudded like the . . . !
Riddle him with lethal pips!

I would not have you age. I swear
I would not have you filter
Dust in the sun, unless you – like the wind –
      Will dance
The tree
      Pray
Pebbles
      Chant
Night
Dance glad anguish of the mother rites,
Unravel seeds, the stranger essence
Sprung from your goodness. I would you
Thus, never never old.

ABIKU

Wanderer child. It is the same child who dies and returns again and again to plague the mother – Yoruba belief.

In vain your bangles cast
Charmed circles at my feet
I am Abiku, calling for the first
And the repeated time.

Must I weep for goats and cowries
For palm oil and the sprinkled ash?
Yams do not sprout in amulets
To earth Abiku's limbs.

So when the snail is burnt in his shell,
Whet the heated fragment, brand me
Deeply on the breast – you must know him
When Abiku calls again.

I am the squirrel teeth, cracked
The riddle of the palm; remember
This, and dig me deeper still into
The god's swollen foot.

Once and the repeated time, ageless
Though I puke, and when you pour
Libations, each finger points me near
The way I came, where

The ground is wet with mourning
White dew suckles flesh-birds
Evening befriends the spider, trapping
Flies in wine-froth;

Night, and Abiku sucks the oil
From lamps. Mothers! I'll be the
Suppliant snake coiled on the doorstep
Yours the killing cry.

The ripest fruit was saddest;
Where I crept, the warmth was cloying.
In silence of webs, Abiku moans, shaping
Mounds from the yolk.

TO MY FIRST WHITE HAIRS

Hirsute hell chimney-spouts, black thunderthroes
confluence of coarse cloudfleeces – my head sir! –
    scourbrush
in bitumen, past fossil beyond fingers of light – until . . . !

Sudden sprung as corn stalk after rain, watered milk weak;
as lightning shrunk to ant's antenna, shrivelled
off the febrile sight of crickets in the sun –

THREE WHITE HAIRS! frail invaders of the undergrowth
interpret time. I view them, wired wisps, vibrant coiled
beneath a magnifying glass, milk-thread presages

Of the hoary phase. Weave then, weave o quickly weave
your sham veneration. Knit me webs of winter sagehood,
nightcap, and the fungoid sequins of a crown.

POST MORTEM

there are more functions to a freezing plant
than stocking beer; cold biers of mortuaries
submit their dues, harnessed – glory be! –

is the cold hand of death . . .
his mouth was cotton filled, his man-pike
shrunk to sub-soil grub

his head was hollowed and his brain
on scales – was this a trick to prove
fore-knowledge after death?

his flesh confesses what has stilled
his tongue; masked fingers think from him
to learn, how not to die.

let us love all things of grey; grey slabs
grey scalpel, one grey sleep and form,
grey images.

For Women

SONG: DESERTED MARKETS

To a Paris night

Deserted markets
Runnels of rain
Seeds fill your gutters
And a long night of pain.

Let me stammer my life
Down your endless lane
The night is for dreaming
And a long bed of pain.

My soul shall be dry
In an ebony grain
Keep it from sprouting
In a stranger's pain.

A night for a life
Dawn hastens in vain
A white bird she comes
And gobbles the grain

For night flowed between
Moon-breasts of pain
And the dew leaves no mark
Where my head has lain.

PSALM

the seeds have ripened fast my love
and the milk is straining at the pods

the ever-eager thought is chaste
at the ruin of your corn-stalk waist

swaddlings of my gratitude
stir within your plenitude.

moist the quickening consciousness
scaled in warm mis-shapenness

ivory granaries are filled
a prize of pain will be fulfilled

bright stream from unbroken springs
threads of ever linking rings

sealed in earth your sanctuary
yields to light; and a mystery

>   of pulses and the stranger life
>   comes to harvest and release
>   the germ and life exegesis
>   inspiration of your genesis.

HER JOY IS WILD

Her joy is wild, wild
Wave-breaking she proclaims,
Your strong teeth will weaken
If you nibble the rind.

Her strength is wild, wild
Wild as the love that sings –
This is the last-born; give me
A joyful womb to bind.

The hour is wild, wild
Denies the wispy moments. Yet
When the fist is loosened, when
The knot is cut, you'll find

Skeins of hair. Wild, wild
Her laughter, dreaming that the tribe
Had slain the senile chieftain
That the rite – was kind.

Her words are wild, wild
Shell the future, place the nut
Between my teeth – and I denied her
Nothing, maimed on her vision of the blind.

BLACK SINGER

(for Marge, New York)

Cold wreath of vine, darkly
Coiled about the night; echoes deep within
Bled veins of autumn

A votive vase, her throat
Poured many souls as one; how dark
The wine became the night.

Fleshed from out disjointed, out from
The sidewalk hurt of sirens, a darkling
Pool of wine shivers

In light shrapnels, and do you ask
How *is* the wine tonight? Dark, lady
Dark in token of the deeper wounds

Full again of promises
Of the deep and silent wounds
Of cruel phases of the darksome wine

Song, O Voice, is lonely envoy
Night a runnel for the wine's indifferent flow.

BRINGER OF PEACE

You come as light rain not to quench
But question out the pride of fire
Watchlight to my peace, within and out
Unguarded moments and the human hours.

You come as light rain, swift to soothe
The rent in earth with deft intrusion
To test your peace on a hiss of ashes
Your sky of lakes on thirsts of embers

Yet fires that hold the beast at bay
Inclose, with all accomplishments of rage
The inborn howl, proud lacerations
Futile vaults at high bounds of the pit

This cunning sift of mild aggression, then
Is your rain, a tacit lie of stillness
A smile to test the python's throes, a touch
To bring the bowstring's nerve to rest.

TO ONE IN LABOUR

For Segi

In silent spaces of the firebrush
Mud regurgitations of the ant
Break air and pollen grain.
The architects

Of spathe and spire survive
Subversions of the human tread
Or mind, some to labour some to yield
A queen her labour

But they build. And I think
Gestation is a Queen insealed
In the cathedral heart, dead lovers round
Her nave of life.

Departed now, the master masons. Desolate
Wonder of you and me, mud spires
Thrust inviolate against colonnades
Of heartwood. Within,

A Queen preparing. Alas for dead lovers
And the silent shrine of pain. In solitude
Of catacombs the lethal arc contracts, my love –
Of your secretions.

BY LITTLE LOVING

After Thomas Blackburn

By little loving, once, I sought
To conquer pain, a bank of bleached
Shells kept floods at bay – once
By little wisdoms, sought the welcome drought.

By little dreaming, once, I kept
My feet from flowered paths. I bared
The night of stealth, watched thwarted
Winds beat cycles, deafened as a crypt.

The paradox of crowds set a marble wall
Where I fled for keeping. Loneliness feeds
On open faces – once by little seeing, fell
To the still centre, off the ruptured wheel

Of blood. And this, the accident of flesh I hailed
Man's eternal lesson – by little yearning to unwind
Cords of closeness. Enough, I swore, the wear
Of pulses, stretch of flesh hunger hourly howled.

I knew redemption in the truth of hate
Yet, fled the careful balance; once,
By little spending I had built
A hoard of peace, yet wondered at the hurt.

They kept vigil long, the winds and the stilled
Night rage, and the tread of waters proved a lie
Bursting from within ... once, by little kindling, I
Fell to dying, phoenix of each pyre forestalled.

Grey Seasons

I THINK IT RAINS

I think it rains
That tongues may loosen from the parch
Uncleave roof-tops of the mouth, hang
Heavy with knowledge

I saw it raise
The sudden cloud, from ashes. Settling
They joined in a ring of grey; within,
The circling spirit

Oh it must rain
These closures on the mind, binding us
In strange despairs, teaching
Purity of sadness

And how it beats
Skeined transparencies on wings
Of our desires, searing dark longings
In cruel baptisms

Rain-reeds, practised in
The grace of yielding, yet unbending
From afar, this your conjugation with my earth
Bares crouching rocks.

PRISONER

Grey, to the low grass cropping
Slung, wet-lichened, wisps from such
Smoke heaviness, elusive of thin blades
Curl inward to the earth, breed
The grey hours,

And days, and years, for do not
The wise grey temples we shall build
To febrile years, here begin – not
In tears and ashes, but on the sad mocking
Threads, compulsive of the hour?

In the desert wildness, when, lone cactus,
Cannibal in his love – even amidst the
Crag and gorge, the leap and night tremors
Even as the potsherd stayed and the sandstorm
Fell – intimations came.

In the whorled centre of the storm, a threnody
But not from this. For that far companion,
Made sudden stranger when the wind slacked
And the centre fell, grief. And the stricken
Potsherd lay, disconsolate – intimations then

But not from these. He knew only
Sudden seizure. And time conquest
Bound him helpless to each grey essence.
Nothing remained if pains and longings
Once, once set the walls; sadness
Closed him, rootless, lacking cause.

SEASON

Rust is ripeness, rust,
And the wilted corn-plume;
Pollen is mating-time when swallows
Weave a dance
Of feathered arrows
Thread corn-stalks in winged
Streaks of light. And, we loved to hear
Spliced phrases of the wind, to hear
Rasps in the field, where corn-leaves
Pierce like bamboo slivers.

Now, garnerers we
Awaiting rust on tassels, draw
Long shadows from the dusk, wreathe
Dry thatch in wood-smoke. Laden stalks
Ride the germ's decay – we await
The promise of the rust.

NIGHT

Your hand is heavy, Night, upon my brow
I bear no heart mercuric like the clouds, to dare
Exarcerbation from your subtle plough.

Woman as a clam, on the far crescent
I saw your jealous eye quench the sea's
Fluorescence, dance on the pulse incessant

Of the waves. And I stood drained
Submitting like the sands, blood and brine
Coursing to the roots. Night, you rained

Serrated shadows through dank leaves
Till, bathed in warm suffusion of your dappled cells
Sensations pained me, faceless, silent night thieves.

Hide me now, when night children haunt the earth –
I must hear none. These misted calls will yet
Undo me, naked, unbidden, at Night's muted birth.

FADO SINGER

For Amalia Roderiguez

My skin is pumiced to a fault
I am down to hair-roots, down to fibre filters
Of the raw tobacco nerve

Your net is spun of sitar strings
To hold the griefs of gods: I wander long
In tear vaults of the sublime

Queen of night torments, you strain
Sutures of song to bear imposition of the rites
Of living and of death. You

Pluck strange dirges from the storm
Sift rare stones from ashes of the moon, and ride
Night errands to the throne of anguish

Oh there is too much crush of petals
For perfume, too heavy tread of air on mothwing
For a cup of rainbow dust

Too much pain, oh midwife at the cry
Of severance, fingers at the cosmic cord, too vast
The pains of easters for a hint of the eternal.

I would be free of your tyranny, free
From sudden plunges of the flesh in earthquake
Beyond all subsidence of sense

I would be free from headlong rides
In rock reams and volcanic veins, drawn by dark steeds
On grey melodic reins.

October '66

IKEJA, FRIDAY, FOUR O'CLOCK

They were but gourds for earth to drink therefrom
The laden trucks, mirage of breath and form

Unbidden offering on the lie of altars
A crop of wrath when hands retract and reason falters

No feast but the eternal retch of human surfeit
No drink but dregs at reckoning of loss and profit

Let nought be wasted, gather up for the recurrent session
Loaves of lead, lusting in the sun's recession.

HARVEST OF HATE

So now the sun moves to die at mid-morning
And laughter wilts on the lips of wine
The fronds of palm are savaged to a bristle
And rashes break on kernelled oil

The hearth is pocked with furnacing of teeth
The air is heavy with rise of incense
For wings womb-moist from the sanctuary of nests
Fall, unfledged to the tribute of fire.

Now pay we forfeit on old abdications
The child dares flames his fathers lit
And in the briefness of too bright flares
Shrivels a heritage of blighted futures

There has been such a crop in time of growing
Such tuneless noises when we longed for sighs
Alone of petals, for muted swell of wine-buds
In August rains, and singing in green spaces.

MASSACRE, OCTOBER '66

Written in Tegel

Shards of sunlight touch me here
Shredded in willows. Through stained-glass
Fragments on the lake I sought to reach
A mind at silt-bed

The lake stayed cold
I swam in an October flush of dying leaves
The gardener's labour flew in seasoned scrolls
Lettering the wind

Swept from painted craft
A mockery of waves remarked this idyll sham
I trod on acorns; each shell's detonation
Aped the skull's uniqueness.

Came sharper reckoning –
This favoured food of hogs cannot number high
As heads still harshly crop to whirlwinds
I have briefly fled

The oak rains a hundred more
A kind confusion to arithmetics of death:
Time to watch autumn the removal man
Dust down rare canvases

To let a loud resolve of passion
Fly to a squirrel, burnished light and copper fur
A distant stance without the lake's churchwindows
And for a stranger, love.

A host of acorns fell, silent
As they are silenced all, whose laughter
Rose from such indifferent paths, oh God
They are not strangers all

Whose desecration mocks the word
Of peace – *salaam aleikun* – not strangers any
Brain of thousands pressed asleep to pig fodder –
Shun pork the unholy – cries the priest.

I borrow seasons of an alien land
In brotherhood of ill, pride of race around me
Strewn in sunlit shards. I borrow alien lands
To stay the season of a mind.

CIVILIAN AND SOLDIER

My apparition rose from the fall of lead,
Declared, 'I'm a civilian.' It only served
To aggravate your fright. For how could I
Have risen, a being of this world, in that hour
Of impartial death! And I thought also: nor is
Your quarrel of this world.

                     You stood still
For both eternities, and oh I heard the lesson
Of your training sessions, cautioning –
Scorch earth behind you, do not leave
A dubious neutral to the rear. Reiteration
Of my civilian quandry, burrowing earth
From the lead festival of your more eager friends
Worked the worse on your confusion, and when
You brought the gun to bear on me, and death
Twitched me gently in the eye, your plight
And all of you came clear to me.

                     I hope some day
Intent upon my trade of living, to be checked
In stride by *your* apparition in a trench,
Signalling, I am a soldier. No hesitation then
But I shall shoot you clean and fair
With meat and bread, a gourd of wine
A bunch of breasts from either arm, and that
Lone question – do you friend, even now, know
What it is all about?

FOR FAJUYI

Honour late restored, early ventured to a trial
Of Death's devising. Flare too rare
Too brief, chivalric steel
Redeems us living, springs the lock of Time's denial

Out from miser earth, thrust from dark, a mystery kernel
Latent till the stress of storms
Sudden soared a miracle of boughs
Recreative temper as the sun's, diurnal.

Feet will not record timbres of iron spines –
Pass over: journeys must end.
Home, forgotten is the bridge
Gold dust in the air, sunk the burdened beam of mines

Weeds triumph. Weeds prowl the path of sandals
Thonged to mountains, thonged
To foundries of futures
Kilns fall tepid, bled by feeble candles

Weeds triumph. What goals for pilgrim feet
But to a dearth of wills
To hills and terraces of gods
Echoes for voices, shadows for the lonely feat.

Flowers thronged his feet whose prints were flagstones
Garlands wither, weeds abide
Who seeks breath of him
Tread the span of bridges, look not down to gravestones.

MALEDICTION

For her who rejoiced

Unsexed, your lips
have framed a life curse
shouting joy where all
the human world
shared in grief's humility.

May this pattern be your life
preserve; that when hearts
are set alive in joy's communion,

a sky of flies in blood-gore
press upon and smear you wholly,

a sky of scab-blacked tears
glut but never slake

those lips
crossed in curse corrugations
thin slit in spittle silting
and bile-blown tongue
pain plagued, a mock man plug
wedged in waste womb-ways
a slime slug slewed in sewage
orogbo ẹgan, gẹgẹ l'ẹkẹ arugbo . . .

Giggles fill the water-hole
Offsprings by you abandoned,
And afterbirth, at crossroads

So when the world grieves, rejoice
Call to them in laughter, beat
Wilted welts on your breasts *bata*
To hyenas of the wastes

even thus
for your children
and your children's
children

that their throats laugh Amen
on your bier, and carousing hooves
raise dust to desecrated dust – Amen.

Preface to IDANRE

Idanre was born of two separate halves of the same experience. The first was a visit to the rockhills of that name, a god-suffused grazing of primal giants and mastodons, petrified through some strange history, suckled by mists and clouds. Three years later and some two hundred miles away, a rainstorm rived apart the intervening years and space, leaving a sediment of disquiet which linked me to lingering, unresolved sensations of my first climb up Idanre. I abandoned my work – it was middle of the night – and walked. *Idanre* is the record of that walk through wet woods on the outskirts of Molete, a pilgrimage to Idanre in company of presences such as dilate the head and erase known worlds. We returned at dawn, the sun was rising just below the hut where we had sheltered on the outward journey. The palm wine girl still waited, the only other human being awake in the vast prescient night, yet an eternal presence whose charity had earthed me from the sublimating essence of the night.

There was a final, postscript image. The rainstorm was the first of the season, yet it had the breath of harvest from the first thunderclap. And as the sun rose over a tarmac hill, the year's harvest followed it in extravagant procession, rich, glorious, sensuous with life.

I took my leave of her, my companions had vanished, I returned home wet from overladen boughs, brittle as the herald lightning to a storm. By nightfall that same day, *Idanre* was completed. It has remained much the same over two years, only the occasional change of a word or a line, little more.

Idanre lost its mystification early enough. As events gathered pace and unreason around me I recognised it as part of a pattern of awareness which began when I wrote *A Dance of the Forests*. In detail, in the human context of my society, *Idanre* has made abundant sense. (The town of Idanre itself was the first to cut its bridge, its only link with the rest of the region during the uprising of October '65.) And since then, the bloody origin of Ogun's pilgrimage has been, in true cyclic manner most bloodily re-enacted. Still awaited is that postscript image of dawn, contained even in the beginning, the brief sun-led promise of earth's forgiveness.

Idanre

Gone, and except for horsemen briefly
Thawed, lit in deep cloud mirrors, lost
The skymen of Void's regenerate Wastes
Striding vast across
My still inchoate earth

The flaming corkscrew etches sharp affinities
(No dream, no vision, no delirium of the dissolute)
When roaring vats of an unstoppered heaven deluge
Earth in fevered distillations, potent with
The fire of the axe-handed one

And greys are violent now, laced with
Whiteburns, tremulous in fire tracings
On detonating peaks. Ogun is still on such
Combatant angles, poised to a fresh descent
Fiery axe-heads fly about his feet

In these white moments of my god, plucking
Light from the day's effacement, the last ember
Glows in his large creative hand, savage round
The rebel mane, ribbed on ridges, crowded in corridors
Low on his spiked symbols

He catches Sango in his three-fingered hand
And runs him down to earth. Safe shields my eaves
This night, I have set the Iron One against
All wayward bolts. Rumours rise on grey corrugations,
The hearth is damped

In gale breaths of the silent blacksmith
Cowls of ashes sweep about his face. Earth

Clutches at the last rallying tendrils
A tongue-tip trembles briefly and withdraws
The last lip of sky is sealed

And no one speaks of secrets in this land
Only, that the skin be bared to welcome rain
And earth prepare, that seeds may swell
And roots take flesh within her, and men
Wake naked into harvest-tide.

II   . . . AND AFTER

He comes, who scrapes no earthdung from his feet
He comes again in Harvest, the first of reapers
Night is our tryst when sounds are clear
And silences ring pure tones as the pause
Of iron bells

 At pilgrims' rest beneath Idanre Hill
 The wine-girl, dazed from divine dallying
 Felt wine-skeins race in fire-patterns within her
 Her eyes queried, what then are you? At such hour
 Why seek what on the hills?

And she swam, an eel into the shadows, felt her limbs
Grow live, the torrents ran within and flooded us
A gourd rose and danced between – without
The night awaited celebration of the crops –
She took, and held it to her womb.

Calm, beyond interpreting, she sat and in her grace
Shared wine with us. The quiet of the night
Shawled us together, secure she was in knowledge
Of that night's benediction. Ogun smiled his peace
Upon her, and we rose

The sky cracked halfways, a greying skull
On blooded highways. I turned, vapours rose
From sodden bitumen and snaked within
Her wrap of indigo, her navel misted over
A sloe bared from the fruit

Darkness veiled her little hills poised
Twin nights against the night, pensive points
In the leer of lightning, and sadness filled
The lone face of the wine-girl; the thatch
Ran rivulets between her breasts.

Harvest night, and time to walk with fruit
Between your lips, on psalming feet. We walked
Silently across a haze of corn, and Ogun
Teased his ears with tassels, his footprints
Future furrows for the giant root

His head was lost among palm towers
And power pylons. Through aeons of darkness rode the
    stone
Of whirling incandescence, and cables danced
In writhing ecstasies, point to point, wart to wart
Of electric coils

The unit kernel atomised, presaging new cohesions
Forms at metagenesis. Ogun lay on tension wires
Slung in hammock, sail-wing birds of night

Nested in his armpits, through pylon rungs flew
Braids of veins, nerved wings and sonic waves

In the blasting of the seed, in the night-birds'
Instant discernment, in the elemental fusion, seed
To current, shone the godhead essence;
One speeds his captive bolts on filaments
Spun of another's forge. And we

Have honeycombed beneath his hills, worked red earth
Of energies, quarrying rare and urgent ores and paid
With wrecks of last year's suppers, paved his roads
With shells, milestones of breathless bones –
Ogun is a demanding god.

We walked through broken braids of steel
And fallen acrobats. The endless safety nets
Of forests prove a green deception
Fated lives ride on the wheels of death when,
The road waits, famished

Cave and castle, shrine and ghostly grottos
Playthings now of children, shades
For browsing goats. The wheels have fallen
To looters and insurance men, litigant on
Spare part sales and terms of premium

The weeds grow sinuous through gaunt corrosions
Skeletons of speed, earth mounds raised towards
Their seeming exhumation; growth is greener where
Rich blood has spilt; brain and marrow make
Fat manure with sheep's excrement

As the First Boulder, as the errant wheel
Of the death chariot, as the creation snake

Spawned tail in mouth, wind chisels and rain pastes
Rust from steel and bones, wake dormant seeds
And suspended lives. I heard

The silence yield to substance. They rose,
The dead whom fruit and oil await
On doorstep shrine and road, their lips
Moist from the first flakes of harvest rain –
Even gods remember dues.

Ogun, godfather of all souls who by road
Made the voyage home, made his being welcome
Suffused in new powers of night, my skin
Grew light with eyes; I watched them drift away
To join the gathering presences

Tomorrow they preside, guests unseen
To whom the rams will bow, and with open throats
Quench totemic thirsts, thirst of earth
The hems of hidden voices brush all feet
This night, dew-wet with departed breaths

> *And to the one whose feet were wreathed*
> *In dark vapours from earth's cooling pitch*
> *I earth my being, she who has felt rain's probing*
> *Vines on night's lamp-post, priestess at fresh shrines*
> *Sacred leaf whose hollow gathers rains*

Vast grows the counterpane of nights since innocence
Of apocalyptic skies, when thunderous shields clashed
Across the heights, when bulls leapt cloud humps and
Thunders opened chasms end to end of fire:
The sky a slate of scoured lettering

Of widening wounds eclipsed in smoke, scabbed
From a pale cauterising hand to a jewelled crucifix
Seared in agonic purities. And except
A *certain* knowledge named it the apocalypse, it stayed
Portents in unquiet nights

Where sprang armoured beasts, unidentifiable,
Nozzles of flames, tails of restive gristles
Banners of saints, cavalcades of awesome hosts
Festival of firevales, crush of starlode
And exploding planets

Whorls of intemperate steel, triangles of cabal
In rabid spheres, iron bellows at volcanic tunnels
Easters in convulsions, urged by energies
Of light millenniums, crusades, empires and revolution
Damnations and savage salvations

Later, diminutive zebras raced on track edges
Round the bed, dwarfs blew on royal bugles
A gaunt *ogboni* raised his staff and vaulted on
A zebra's back, galloped up a quivering nose –
A battle with the suffocating shrouds

Opalescent pythons oozed tar coils
Hung from rafters thrashing loops of gelatine
The world was choked in wet embrace
Of serpent spawn, waiting Ajantala's rebel birth
Monster child, wrestling pachyderms of myth,

> *And at the haven of a distant square*
> *Of light, hope's sliver from vile entombment*
> *She waited, caryatid at the door of sanctuary*

Her hands were groves of peace, Oya's forehead
Dipped to pools and still hypnotic springs

And now she is a dark sheath freed
From Ogun's sword, her head of tapered plaits
A casque of iron filigree, a strength
Among sweet reeds and lemon bushes, palm
And fragrances of rain

The night glowed violet about his head
He reached a large hand to tension wires
And plucked a string; earth was a surreal bowl
Of sounds and mystic timbres, his fingers
Drew warring elements to a union of being

And taught the veins to dance, of earth of rock
Of tree, sky, of fire and rain, of flesh of man
And woman. Ogun is the god that ventures first
His path one loop of time, one iron coil
Earth's broken rings were healed

III   PILGRIMAGE

We stood upon Idanre's columns and he fell,
The Iron One, to grieving. His breast
The crown of Idanre Hill, stooped, pressed upon
By clouds dark with moulted deeds
And accusing forms

Union they had known until the Boulder
Rolling down the hill of the Beginning

Shred the kernel to a million lights.
A traitor's heart rejoiced, the gods' own slave
Dirt-covered from the deed

Man's passage, pre-ordained, self-ordered winds
In reconstruction. (Piecemeal was *their* deft
Re-birth, a cupped shell of tortoise, staggered
Tile tegument;) And the monolith of man searches still
A blind hunger in the road's hidden belly.

Idanre's boulder complex rose before us and he grieved
The veins were dying in the flesh of earth
Bled of all lustre, the lodes were crumbled
And the fires fallen to ashes. Light, more
Than human frame can bear

Set flanges to a god, control had slipped
Immortal grasp. On the hills of Idanre memories
Grieved him, my Hunter god, Vital
Flint of matter, total essence split again
On recurrent boulders

This road have I trodden in a time beyond
Memory of fallen leaves, beyond
Thread of fossil on the slate, yet I must
This way again. Let all wait the circulation
Of time's acrobat, who pray

For dissolution: the chronicle abides in clay texts
And fossil textures. I followed fearful, archives
Of deities heaved from primal burdens; Ogun
Sought the season's absolution, on the rocks of genesis
Night weighed huge about me

And I walked in footprints of a god
Whose knees struck sparks to burn the night
Brushing rocks in self-rage up the hill, up
His hermitage in rockshields lost in cloud
Caverns, Outcast Deity!

IV   THE BEGINNING

Low beneath rockshields, home of the Iron One
The sun had built a fire within
Earth's heartstone. Flames in fever fits
Ran in rock fissures, and hill surfaces
Were all aglow with earth's transparency

   Orisa-nla, Orunmila, Esu, Ifa were all assembled
   Defeated in the quest to fraternise with man

Wordlessly he rose, sought knowledge in the hills
Ogun the lone one saw it all, the secret
Veins of matter, and the circling lodes
Sango's spent thunderbolt served him a hammer-head
His fingers touched earth-core, and it yielded

   To think, a mere plague of finite chaos
   Stood between the gods and man

He made a mesh of elements, from stone
Of fire in earthfruit, the womb of energies
He made an anvil of the peaks, and kneaded
Red clay for his mould. In his hand the Weapon
Gleamed, born of the primal mechanic

And this pledge he gave the heavens
I will clear a path to man

His task was ended, he declined the crown
Of deities, sought retreat in heights. But Ire
Laid skilled siege to divine withdrawal. Alas
For diplomatic arts, the Elders of Ire prevailed;
He descended, and they crowned him king

Who speaks to me in chance recesses
Who guides the finger's eye

Now he climbs in reparation, who annointed
Godhead in carnage, O let heaven loose the bolts
Of last season's dam for him to lave his fingers
Merely, and in the heady line of blood
Vultures drown. Merely,

And in the lungstreams of depleted pastures
Earth is flattened. O the children of Ogun
Reaped red earth that harvest, rain
Is children's reeds and the sky a bird-pond
Until my god has bathed his hands

Who brings a god to supper, guard him well
And set his place with a long bamboo pole

Ogun is the lascivious god who takes
Seven gourdlets to war. One for gunpowder,
One for charms, two for palm wine and three
Air-sealed in polished bronze make
Storage for his sperms

My god Ogun, orphans' shield, his home
Is terraced hills self-surmounting to the skies

Ogun path-maker, he who goes fore where other gods
Have turned. Shield of orphans, was your shield
In-spiked that day on sheltering lives?

Yet had he fled when his primal task was done
Fugitive from man and god, ever seeking hills
And rock bounds. Idanre's granite offered peace
And there he dwelt until the emissaries came –
Lead us king, and warlord.

  Who speaks to me I cannot tell
  Who guides the hammer's flight

Gods drowse in boredom, and their pity
Is easy roused with lush obsequious rites
Because the rodent nibbled somewhat at his yam,
The farmer hired a hunter, filled him with wine
And thrust a firebrand in his hand

  We do not burn the woods to trap
  A squirrel; we do not ask the mountain's
  Aid, to crack a walnut.

v   THE BATTLE

  Overtaking fugitives
  A rust-red swarm of locusts
  Dine off grains

  Quick proboscis
  Find the coolers
  Soon the wells are dry

Presumptuous eaves
Of safety, hang stark
Only this shelter for
Returning men

This filigree
Of foliage veins
Lets in the moon's
Leprous sneer

Truth peeps in
On every side
Welcomes the wind
From frightened men

Ah but his hands cleave frenetic
To the jig! Prestidigitator god midst head
And limb, they poise a full eternity
And falling, bounce to rare wave-lengths

His sword possesses all

There are air-paths unknown to human sight
Arabesques of light, a keen maze where all
Who seek strategic outlets find
O Iron One

The shortest cut

Storms strain his mighty chest, his nipples
Glow with blackness, from hair-roots
Spit black jets of flames. Tall he rises to the hills
His head a rain-cloud has eclipsed the sun
His nostrils blow visible

Exhalations as twin-flues through clouds
There are myriad lesser motes in flight
And leaping mists. Never to his ears,
Never to him comes the cry of men
In sweet lather of death.

> Lord of all witches, divine hunter
> Your men Ogun, your men!

His sword an outer crescent of the sun
No eye can follow it, no breath draws
In wake of burning vapour. Still they cry

> Your men Ogun! Your men!

This blade he forged, its progress
Never falters, rivulets on it so swift
The blood forgets to clot

There are falling ears of corn
And ripe melons tumble from the heads
Of noisy women, crying

> Lust-blind god, gore-drunk Hunter
> Monster deity, you destroy your men!

He strides sweat encrusted
Bristles on risen tendons
Porcupine and barbed. Again he turns
Into his men, a butcher's axe
Rises and sinks

> Behind it, a guest no one
> Can recall.

Where do we seek him, they asked?
Where conflict rages, where sweat
Is torrents of rain, where clear springs
Of blood fill one with longing
As the rush of wine

    So there they sought
    And there they find him

And youth that came to teeth on the encounter?
What greater boon for the fledgeling! The wings
Of a god enclose him wholly, there is
No room for air

    Smothered in wind-deafness
    Blinded in light-paths of suns

There are air-beams unfelt by human breath
Unseen by sight, intangible. Whose throat
Draws breath in a god's preserve
Breathes the heart of fire

    Murderer, stay your iron hand
    Your men lie slain – Cannibal!

Ay, ring summons on the deafened god
His fingers sow red earth. His being incarnate
Bathes in carnage, anoints godhead
In carnage

To bring a god to supper is devout, yet
A wise host keeps his distance till
The Spirit One has dined his fill. What mortal
Brands a platter with an awesome name,

Or feeds him morsels choice without
Gauntlets of iron. A human feast
Is indifferent morsel to a god.

A lethal arc
Completes full circle

Unsheathed
The other half
Of fire

Incinerates
All subterfuge
Enthrones
The fatal variant

The rodent's nose explored the shadows
Found sweat and gangrene
Smell the same to a skin tailor. Beyond
A prayer for sunshine, what interest
Does a stagnant pool pretend
To a river in flood?

The rams
Are gathered to the stream
For blessing

Hour of prayer
And curved horns curve
Into hearts of the faithful

The priest
Cleansed his fingers
In new springs

And drank.
All routes led
To the sacrificial knife

That dawn
On the plains of prayer
A flat stream
And new springs

All prayers were one
To the Iron One

Let each seek wisdom where he can, life's
Puppetry creaks round me hourly
Trunks and motions in masquerade grotesques
Post-mortem is for quacks and chroniclers
Who failed at divination

Esu, my little prince of games sat
On his head, and he was deaf to identifying
Cries. Too late came warning that a god
Is still a god to men, and men are one
When knowledge comes, of death.

And they were cast adrift, without
Direction for new prayers, their cry
For partial succour brought a total hand
That smothered life on crimson plains
With too much answering

The royal baobab
Dances with the head alone
To a wind's possession

Who has no roots
In earth
Deep in rock-chambers . . .

Its eardrops
Makes a wine-cup
Of my sheltering head

When the wind insists

Who has no root
In earth
Flee the shelter
Of a god possessed

Light filled me then, intruder though
I watched a god's excorsis; clearly
The blasphemy of my humanity rose accusatory
In my ears, and understanding came
Of a fatal condemnation

And in that moment broke his crust of separation
And the blood-scales of his eyes. A wind's insinuation
Lowered his arm, scattering blood-fogs; revealed
The vessel that was singly cast, crepitate
In orphan sherds.

He recognised the pattern of the spinning rock
And Passion slowly yielded to remorse

Melted then the wine-logged eyes, embers
No gourd ever assuaged, kernels fire-red
On blacksmith tongs. A god knows no comforter
And I am not prone to pity. Divine outcast
And your captains bold?

Did not your primal science reave discs
Of light, a keen maze for pupils of the forge?

Too late for joy, the Hunter stayed his hand
The chute of truth opened from red furnaces
And Ogun stayed his hand

Truth, a late dawn,

Life, the two-cowrie change of the dealer
In trinkets lay about him in broken threads
Oh the squirrel ran up an *iroko* tree
And the hunter's chase
Was ended.

VI   RECESSIONAL

I walked upon a deserted night before
The gathering of Harvest, companion at a god's
Pre-banquet. The hills of Idanre beckoned me
As who would yield her secrets, locked
In sepulchral granite.

Sightless eyes prayed haste upon
His slow descent, incurious to behold
The claws of day rip wide the weakened shutters
Of a mind divine. Who knows from what savage
Tumours, floods a god's remorse.

A child averts his eye from an elder's
Nakedness; pursued by blood in his lone descent

The silence said, Go your way, and if
Our dead pass you on your way, smooth their path
To where is home.

He who had sought heights inaccessible to safeguard
The vital flint, heard, not voices whom the hour
Of death had made all one, nor futile flight
But the assertive act of Atunda, and he was shamed
In recognition of the grim particular

It will be time enough, and space, when we are dead
To be a spoonful of the protoplasmic broth
Cold in wind-tunnels, lava flow of nether worlds
Deaf to thunder blind to light, comatose
In one omni-sentient cauldron

Time enough to abdicate to astral tidiness
The all in one, superior annihilation of the poet's
Diversity – oh how his words condemn him, who declared
A fragrance in the stars, plunged to the mind's abyss
In contemplation of a desert well

I shall remain in knowledge of myself, as Idanre's
Bold concretion at the night, wear its anonymity
Not dissolution. For who will stand beside
The god, who welcome rain, who celebrate Idanre
Iterate carbuncle of Night?

Who, inhesion of disparate senses, of matter
Thought, entities and motions, who sleep-walk
Incensed in Nirvana – a code of Passage
And the Night – who, cloyed, a mote in homogeneous gel
Touch the living and the dead?

Rather, may we celebrate the stray electron, defiant
Of patterns, celebrate the splitting of the gods
Cannonisation of the strong hand of a slave who set
The rock in revolution – and the Boulder cannot
Up the hill in time's unwind.

You who have borne the first separation, bide you
Severed still; he who guards the Creative Flint
Walks, purged spirit, contemptuous of womb-yearnings
He shall teach us to ignite our several kilns
And glory in each bronzed emergence.

All hail Saint Atunda, First revolutionary
Grand iconoclast at genesis – and the rest in logic
Zeus, Osiris, Jahweh, Christ in trifoliate
Pact with creation, and the wisdom of Orunmila, Ifa
Divining eyes, multiform

Evolution of the self-devouring snake to spatials
New in symbol, banked loop of the 'Mobius Strip'
And interlock of re-creative rings, one surface
Yet full comb of angles, uni-plane, yet sensuous with
Complexities of mind and motion.

VII   HARVEST

Night sets me free; I suffer skies to sprout
Ebb to full navel in progressive arcs, ocean
Of a million roe, highway of eyes and moth-wings.
Night sets me free, I ride on ovary silences
In the wake of ghosts

Ogun's mantle brushed the leaves, the phase of night
Was mellow wine joined to a dirge
Of shadows, the air withdrew to scything motions
Of his dark-shod feet, seven-ply crossroads
Hands of camwood, breath of indigo

Night sets me free, soft sediments on skin
And sub-soil mind . . . Dawn came gradual, mists
Fell away from rock and honeycomb, Idanre woke
To braided vapours, a dance of seven veils
The septuple god was groom and king.

Mists fell to mote infinities from mountain face
Retrieved, were finely gathered to a sponge
Of froth murmurs in palm veins, he rinsed
The sunrise of his throat in agile wine; I took the sun
In his copper calabash

Dawn, He who had dire reaped
And in wrong season, bade the forests swallow him
And left mankind to harvest. At pilgrim lodge
The wine-girl kept lone vigil, fused still
In her hour of charity

A dawn of bright processions, the sun peacocked
Loud, a new mint of coins. And those were all
The night hours, only the dissipated gourds,
Rain serried floor, fibre walls in parsimonious
Sifting of the sun, and she . . .

Light burnished to a copper earth, cornucopia
Fell in light cascades round her feet. Our paths
Grew solemn as her indrawn eye, bride of Night

Hoard of virgin dawns, expectant grew her distant gaze
And Harvest came, responsive

The first fruits rose from subterranean hoards
First in our vision, corn sheaves rose over hill
Long before the bearers, domes of eggs and flesh
Of palm fruit, red, oil black, froth flew in sun bubbles
Burst over throngs of golden gourds

And they moved towards resorption in His alloy essence
Primed to a fusion, primed to the sun's dispersion
Containment and communion, seed-time and harvest, palm
And pylon, Ogun's road a 'Mobius' orbit, kernel
And electrons, wine to alchemy.

NOTES ON *IDANRE*

I DELUGE ...

    1. axe-handed one   Sango, god of lightning and electricity.

    2. Ogun   God of Iron and metallurgy, Explorer, Artisan, Hunter, God of war, Guardian of the Road, the Creative Essence. His season is harvest and the rains.

    3. Sango   See 1 above.

II ... AND AFTER

    1. wine-girl   Also Oya, once the wife of Ogun, latterly of Sango. (Worn out by Ogun's fearsome nature, she deserted him for Sango.) Also a dead girl, killed in a motor accident.

    2. etc.   This and following stanzas celebrate the fusion of the two essences, Ogun and Sango, already symbolised in the person of their common wife, Oya. Today Ogun of the metallic lore conducts Sango's electricity. The ritual dance of the union is seen sometimes during an electric storm when from high-tension wires leap figures of ecstatic flames. This is the ideal fusion – to preserve the original uniqueness and yet absorb another essence.

    3. etc.   Apocalyptic visions of childhood and other deliriums.

    4. ogboni   Cultic executive of Yoruba society; an elders' conclave, a member.

| 5. Ajantala | Archetype of the rebel child, iconoclast, anarchic, anti-clan, anti-matriarch, virile essence in opposition to womb-domination. |

III THE PILGRIMAGE

| 1. traitor | Atoóda (also called Atunda), slave to first deity. Either from pique or revolutionary ideas he rolled a rock down onto his unsuspecting master, smashing him to bits and creating the multiple godhead. |

IV IN THE BEGINNING

1. Orisa-nla	Head of the deities.
Orunmila	Sky-God, essence of wisdom.
Esu	God of chance, disruption.
Ifa	Divination and order.

V THE BATTLE

Ogun's day of error. King of Ire against his will, he soon led his men into battle. Drunk with wine and blinded by gore Ogun turned on his own men and slaughtered them. Annually he re-enacts his deed of shame.

VI RECESSIONAL

| 1. Atoóda | See III, 1. |
| 2. Mobius Strip | A mathe-magical ring, infinite in self-re-creation into independent but linked rings and therefore the freest conceivable (to me) symbol of human or divine (e.g. Yoruba, Olympian) relationships. A symbol of optimism also, as it gives the illusion of a 'kink' in the |

circle and a possible centrifugal escape from the eternal cycle of karmas that has become the evil history of man. Only an illusion but a poetic one, for the Mobius strip is a very simple figure of aesthetic and scientific truths and contradictions. In this sense, it is the symbol of Ogun in particular, and an evolution from the tail-devouring snake which he sometimes hangs around his neck and symbolises the doom of repetition. And even if the primal cycle were of good and innocence, the Atoọda of the world deserve praise for introducing the evolutionary 'kink'.

VII HARVEST

1. alchemy

The magic communion of the body, the earth and metals (see Camara Laye's account of his goldsmith father at work). Blood tempers steel, and so may wine.

*A Shuttle
in the
Crypt*

—

The shuttle is a unique species of the caged animal, a restless bolt of energy, a trapped weaver-bird yet charged in repose with unspoken forms and designs. In motion or at rest it is a secretive seed, shrine, kernel, phallus and well of creative mysteries. Self-identification with this essence of innate repletion was a natural weapon to employ against the dangers of an inhuman isolation. It was never a mere poetic conceit; all events, thoughts, dreams, incidental phenomena were, in sheer self-protection perceived and absorbed into the loom-shuttle unity of such an existence.

Except for two or three poems in the section 'Poems of bread and earth' this volume consists of poems written in gaol in spite of the deprivation of reading and writing material in nearly two years of solitary confinement. It is a map of the course trodden by the mind, not a record of the actual struggle against a vegetable existence – that belongs in another place.

Chimes of Silence is central to the entire experience. The passage of five men to and through that travesty of looms, the gallows, was at once harrowing and consoling. Seeing nothing but sealed in a vault which drew in the sounds of it all, it was a private ritual solely for, solely witnessed by me. I listened to an enactment of death in the home of death, to the pulse of a shuttle slowing to its final moment of rest, towards that complete in-gathering of being which a shuttle in repose so palpably is. It was, in this sense, both horror and consolation.

The landscape of the poems is not uncommon; physical details differ, but finally the landscape of the loss of human contact is the same. 'Bearings' which is a topographical preface to the body of *Chimes* etches some of these physical details. Under *Phases of Peril*, 'Conversation at Night' seems at first a strange inclusion, but it was indeed this kind of evocation of events, yielding nothing but past and future evidence of the unchanging nature of humanity which set in process the worst moments of pessimism.

And it was this ever-recurrent awareness, this level of the loss of human contact that proved more corrosive than that purely physical loss upon which the little mind-butchers had based their hope.

WOLE SOYINKA

JULY, 1971

Phases of Peril

O ROOTS!

Roots, be an anchor at my keel
Shore my limbs against the wayward gale

Reach in earth for deep sustaining draughts
Potencies against my endless thirsts

Your surface runnels end in blinds, your courses
Choke on silt, stagnate in human curses

Feet of pilgrims pause by charted pools
Balm seeking. Dipped, their thirsty bowls

Raise bubbles of corruption, sludge
Of evil, graves unlaid to tears or dirge

Roots, I pray you lead away from streams
Of tainted seepage lest I, of these crimes

Partake, from fouled communion earth
In ashes scattered from a common hearth

Roots! lead away from treachery of the dark
From pit of acceptance, from the baited stake

Lend not image to a serpent spawn
Of lures, to monster prodigies of spleen

Do not, pride of sinews tunnel far
In secrets, yet surface close to guilty fear

To grasp of greed, to bane of spittle squalls
On quivers of green-awakening quills.

O Roots, be an anchor at my keel
Cord my thoughts from tensed, rock-suturing reel

Reach in earth to new sustaining draughts
Pierce her timeless hoards with keen-eyed shafts

Flush hours of staleness out to death's
Eternal sump. Arouse the captive breaths

Of springs and vaulted lakes, their waters draw
To seedling hands, to goals on threshing-floor

Roots, be the network of my large
Design, hold to your secret charge

All bedrock architecture raised to heal
Desert cries, desert lacerations; seal

In barks of age, test on battering-rams
Of your granite caps O breaker of dams

Pestle in earth mortar, ringer of chimes
In rock funnels, render mine Time's

Chaplets, and stress to your eternal season
These inward plinths I raise against unreason

Against the dark-sprung moment of the trap
Against the noontide thunderclap!

Pathfinder to the underworld, lead
My feet to core, to kernel seed

Draw me still to crucibles of earth's
Alchemistry, to rock and metal births

To vibrations of your tuning-fork.
Press these palms, that they shall join in talk,

In memories, sights, to blindfold passing ones
Borne to the eternal banquet on wine-tidal runs

Let my hands intertwine with theirs
Clear sap and dark, red flesh and ghost hairs

Cell chains as leaf and limb, vein
Of limb and rock, eyes in womb of grain

To a filter of impulses weave their bones
That combs of my marrow may, in kernel stones

Receive the roots of lightning from the sky
Storing light of their departed eye

Draw to earth all lethal pulses, that my cup
Of hands may echo fiery harmonies, and sup

At wedding-feasts of sky and earth. Thread
My hands to spring-rites, to green hands of the dead.

O Roots Roots. If it Shall Not Withstand!
If it shall cave to wind and choke in sands

Of wilderness, if it shall cinder in flash
Of the dearth-awaited, your coils unleash

Upon the last defence of sluices! The prow
Is pointed to a pull of undertows

A grey plunge in pools of silence, peace
Of bygone voyagers, to the close transforming pass.

Cleansed, they await, the seeker come
To a drought of centres, to slipholds on the climb

And heart may yield to strange upwelling thrusts,
Promising from far to slake immortal thirsts.

CONVERSATION AT NIGHT
WITH A COCKROACH

Come out. Oh have you found me even here
Cockroach? grimed in gloss connivance
Carapaced in age, in cunning, oiled
As darkness, keyed in decoy rasps.
Your subtle feelers probed prize chapters
Drilled perforations on the magic words.
Our maps did not long survive your trails
To mislead, false contours from secretions
Of your poison ducts. Oh you have claws
To leak the day of pity, skin the night
Of love, pierce holes invisible
Within the heart of nature for all
Of good to seep through unnoticed and unmourned.
Saw teeth, dribbling a caress
Of spittle on the wound, you nibbled trust
From the heart of our concerted bond
Yet left the seals intact. Our limbs
And voices carried on to cheers and whirring
Of your fluted wings. But lost
Was the heart of purpose, soiled
Our standard of the awakened hour.

You know to wait out, sleek in dirt
The first fire-arc of regenerate eyes,
Lowered beneath the rotted roots, attuned
To a stale, complacement air. You know what hands
Are sworn to seedling, whose large Visitation
Plants even with the cropping.

Close upon their steps we creep
Cockroach, termite and train
Rooting up even before
The clutching of the germ
Foremost of the jubilating horde
Our voices lead in welcome
Below the joy-froth's endless cressets
We churn our silt of discord
And ours are fingers on the dredge
Working conveyors in reverse.
What could you? What can you?
Why do you light the fires?

In that year's crucible we sought
To force impurities in nationweal
Belly-up, heat-drawn by fires
Of truth. In that year's crucible
We sought to cleanse the faulted lodes
To raise new dwellings pillared on crags
Washed by mountain streams; to reach
Hands around Kaura hills, beyond
Obudu ranges, to dance on rockhills
Through Idanre. We sought to speak
Each to each in accents of trust
Dispersing ancient mists in clean breezes
To clear the path of lowland barriers
Forge new realities, free our earth
Of distorting shadows cast by old
And modern necromancers. No more
Rose cry and purpose, no more the fences
Of deceit, no more perpetuity
Of ancient wrongs.

But we were wise to portents, tuned
As tinsel vanes to the dread approach
Of the Visitation. And while the rumble yet
Was far, we closed, we spread the tentacles.

We knew the tread and heard
The gathering heartbeat of the cyclone heart
And quick our hands to forge coalitions new
Of tried corruptions, East to West, North to South.
Survival was insured in policies to embrace
The full degree of wavering weather vanes.
Our sirens poised inked talons on the open
Cheques, their songs inflamed each hidden longing:

Rest. Rock not our neat foundations
With futile quarrying. Pace pulses
Of your thoughts to cycles as of water-wheels
Dipping with aged ease in wells
Of milk and honey. Journeys end
On cattle hide for restless egrets
And what are desert vistas but the ruins
Of wind-blown pasts, sand-dunes
Of futile energies in wastrel winds
What gain the pangs of distant urges
Surge and spring of migratory power
All come at last to the placid hide
A prodigal's home-coming to the herd.

Weary? Rest, and to distant echoes of
Their evensong I'll lull you with a sweet
Lament of victims. Oh I've crept among them

Even as here, to stare and probe, seeking crumbs
Hidden or fallen. I've tickled out their dreams
With quiet antennae in the dead of night. Listen:

And we had sojourned long among
Our violators, generations of far-flung
Clans, and taken wives among them
And given daughters unto them for wives.
Our offspring knew no land but this
No air, no earth, no loves or death
Only the brittle sky in harmattan
And in due season, rain to waken scrub
A hailstone herald to the rouse
Of hills, echoes in canyons, pastures
In the palm of ranges, moss horizons
On distant ridges, anthill spires for milestones.
We sought no pledges save those dusks of peace
Sung by muezzins to kith and stranger
No stranger horizon than sails of egrets
Breaking on the minarets, we walked among
Baobab landmarks on our uncharted prospects –
And this they call the tree of life! – indeed
We lived in the land of pyramids
Groundnut stacks to a skyline of the first
Exodus – there let all semblance rest –
Nor sea nor river closed upon our assailants
The plague did not plague them. Our firstborn
It was that died.

Peace. The spillage dried with time
We nibbled blood where it had caked
You lit the fires, you, and saw

Your dawn of dawning yield
To our noon of darkness
Half-way up your grove of union
We watched you stumble – mere men
Lose footing on the peaks of deities.
The torch was quenched, the void
Of darkness rang with madness
Each his own priest, quick, easy
The act of sacrifice. We know to wait.
We nibble blood before it cakes.

Night scavengers
Heavy with the season's fruition
Whelped they in laughter
To a moon's decay

Rabid teats
To suckle rivers
A trail of slavering
Coated the whetstones
Waiting the tempering of blades

This was the dew
That fell in night hours
The night contagion

Upon new-forged weapons
In open lairs
Laid for consecration
To the love-feast of the morrow

A round table, board
Of the new abiding – man, ghoul, Cockroach,

Jackal and brood of vile cross-breedings
Broke bread to a loud veneration
Of awe-filled creatures of the wild,
Sat to a feast of love – our pulsing hearts!

Not human faces, hands, were these
That fell upon us, nor was death withheld
Even from children, from the unborn.
And wombs were torn from living women
And eyes of children taken out
On the points of knives and bayonets.
The sky was blotted out in funeral pyres
And the faggots were limbs of the living.
There was no sanctuary, in mosque or chapel,
In surgeries where we fled for healing hands,
On gravestep or in cradle. The hearses
On this day were gravel tippers, smoothly
Functioning upon the leverage of death.
An endless shuttle from rich laden fields
Of slaughter, to hasty pits, dams, ponds
Sewers. And many drew last breath
Beneath the earth, below corrupted waters.
Many, buoyed on the swollen husks
Of past departures, thrashed a dying hope
To banks. Death's face of mockery grinned
And beckoned, rock or pole in hand.
None came living from the floods
Of hate's dark waters.

   I murmured to their riven hearts:
   Yet blood must flow, a living flood
   Bravely guarded, boldly split

A potency to rejuvenate
Mothers-of-all earth, the river's
Endless cycle with the sap
Of trees, wine of palm, oil
Of kernels, lamp-light in rock bearings
Let even as treasures are
An offering to red pulses
Beating to the larger life –
Oh I know my lore, I've heard the poets.

Stale deception. Blasphemer's consolation.
This was death in evil, death without hue
This death wore the cloak of scavengers
Grave-robbers, claws of greed on leathery hands
Blind squeaks in the humid stench
Of usurers' conservation. Death came
In the colour of foul thoughts and whispers
Fouled intentions, colour of calculations
A contrivance to erase the red and black
Of debt and credit, gangrene to discolour
Records for future reckoning, bile to blur
Precision of the mind to past exploitation
A scheming for intestate legacies
Conversions, appropriations, a mine
Of gold-filling in the teeth of death
A colour blindness to red standards
Which tomorrow shall uphold against
The horrors of today.

          They do not bleed
On whom the dunghill falls, nor they
Whose bones are sucked of marrow

In noon perversions of inhuman tongues
They do not bleed whose breaths are stilled
In sludges or sewers, who slither down
To death on the burst tumour of hate's
Inventive mind, through chasms of the flight
Of earth from rites of defilement,
Dark of abomination. They do not bleed
Whose wombs are bared to leprous lust.

Tears are rainfall in the house of death
Softening, purging, purifying. Tears
Are a watering shed to earth's
Unceasing wounds. This death was arid
There was no groan, no sorrowing at the wake –
Only curses. No suffering, for the senses
Were first to die. We died, the world
Turned a blank eye to the sky
And prayed: May Heaven comfort you;
On earth, our fears must teach us silence.

A little stone
Disgorged its tenant. The Cockroach
Spread his wings in a feeble sun
And rasped his saw-teeth. A song
Of triumph rose on deadened air
A feeler probed the awful silence,
Withdrew in foreknowing contentment –

All was well. All was even
As it was in the beginning.

A COBWEB'S TOUCH IN THE DARK

Touching
By moth-eyes on fingers, trailing
Dark vapours of the earth exhaling

Hearing
Voices of our dead in leaves their presences
Have nourished, in more than foliage essences

A skin
Whose hairs are brushed by winds that shade
Spaces where dead memories are laid

A thread
Lays its moment on the flesh, a rime
Of things gone by, a brush of time

It slips
Against the dark, radial and ebb-
line to the heart of the ancestral web.

WHEN SEASONS CHANGE

When seasons change it seems
An age is passed, and all with it
And this old earth has sucked within it
Souls of all living. Time's spectres, they
Evade guardianship of predecessors
They thread their way through rocks
And creviced growths, old, silent vapours.
What seek you, cloud weeds in air
Whose thoughts are old, hoar-rimmed
As sunken eyes on the forgotten face
Of this my hermit earth? They wander on
In whispering parade, full of old hints
Old truths upheld in mirrors of the hour –
A solemn future casts a backward glance
Over drooped shoulders.

                                        The mind
Is banked upon the bankrupt flow
Of wisdoms new. It soars in flight
Upon a dual lift of planes, shifting in cross-winds
A noble slave, air-borne on the cross
Of twin-adherents, equal lift and span –
Knowledge of a deep futility in all
Of far ideas and urgent action – this
The right wing, poise and balance
Wind-drag on – the left, fate, propulsion
Beating wind and homing on the beam
Responsive ever to the present call.

Hailstone summons on the dovecot roof
The drums are here again, flight courses
Tapped on questing minds. The lines are worn
And reading blurred in time's fingerstains.
Shed your hard tears; it is an old earth
Stirring to fresh touch of old pretensions
Throbs of dead passion, chilled rebounds
From sensations of the past, old hands and voices
The blows of battle and the scars, old fences
And the guarded opening of a gate
Old welcomes, the heat of comradeship
And cold betrayal, old sacrifices
The little victories and the greater loss –
Thus, purity of ideals, clarity of vision,
And oh, let innocence have brief mourning –
Old compromises.

Yet this progression has been source
For great truths in spite of stammering
Planes for great building in spite
Of crooked sights, for plastic strength
Despite corrosive fumes of treachery
And spirits grow despite the midwifery
Of dwarfs; spires, rooted in quagmires
Of the human mind rise to purer lights
And wing aloft a salvaged essence
Transcending death, legacy of seasons ...

Ecstasies are brief; it is truth's season
And golden eyelets sink grey hooded
In the ashen hearth of truth. Now moves
A dead recession of the silent host

Whispering judgements, sucking spires
Down to dwarf kennels, liming minds
That took to wing, sighing sinews down
To atrophy: a damp of knowing smiles
At urges of the flesh to a self-release
In transcendencies.

Shrouds of seasons gone, peeled
From time's corpses, mouse-eaten thoughts
You flutter upon solitude in winds
Armed in shrapnels from the shell of vision
Veils on the altar of unplighted troths
Cobweb hangings on the throne of death
In solitude.

TO THE MADMEN OVER THE WALL

Howl, howl
Your fill and overripeness of the heart,
I may not come with you
Companions of the broken buoy
I may not seek
The harbour of your drifting shore.

Your wise withdrawal
Who can blame? Crouched
Upon your ledge of space, do you witness
Ashes of reality drift strangely past?
I fear
Your minds have dared the infinite
And journeyed back
To speak in foreign tongues.

Though walls
May rupture tired seams
Of the magic cloak we share, yet
Closer I may not come
But though I set my ears against
The tune of setting forth, yet, howl
Upon the hour of sleep, tell these walls
The human heart may hold
Only so much despair.

I ANOINT MY FLESH

(Tenth Day of Fast)

I anoint my flesh
Thought is hallowed in the lean
Oil of solitude
I call you forth, all, upon
Terraces of light. Let the dark
Withdraw

I anoint my voice
And let it sound hereafter
Or dissolve upon its lonely passage
In your void. Voices new
Shall rouse the echoes when
Evil shall again arise

I anoint my heart
Within its flame I lay
Spent ashes of your hate –
Let evil die.

Four Archetypes

JOSEPH

(to Mrs Potiphar)

O Mrs Potiphar, your principles
Which I would not embrace you swore
I tried to violate; I see you wave as trophy
Tattered pieces of your masquerade
Of virtue, and call them mine.

Indeed I was not Joseph, a cursing martyr I,
No saint – are saints not moved beyond
Event, their passive valour tuned to time's
Slow unfolding? A time of evils cries
Renunciation of the saintly vision
Summons instant hands of truth to tear
All painted masks, that poison stains thereon
May join and trace the hidden undertows
In sewers of intrigue. Dear Mrs Potiphar
You seek through chaos to bury deep
Your scarlet pottage of guilt, your grim manure
For weeds of sick ambition.

                        Time's slaves
Eunuchs of will wait upon you; sink
Down deep in whitened couch of bones, recline
Today upon tomorrow's hollowed skulls. We,
All whose dreams of fire resolve in light
Wait upon the old ancestor in pursuit
Of truths, and to interpret dreams.

HAMLET

He stilled his doubts, they rose to halt and lame
A resolution on the rack. Passion's flame
Was doused in fear of error, his mind's unease
Bred indulgence to the state's disease

Ghosts embowelled his earth; he clung to rails
In a gallery of abstractions, dissecting tales
As 'told by an idiot'. Passionless he set a stage
Of passion for the guilt he would engage.

Justice despaired. The turn and turn abouts
Of reason danced default to duty's counterpoint
Till treachery scratched the slate of primal clay
Then Metaphysics waived a thought's delay –
It took the salt in the wound, the 'point
Envenom'd too' to steel the prince of doubts.

GULLIVER

Once upon a ship-(of state)-wreck, where
The sun had shrunk the world at last to a true
Stature of deserving – the ant for unit –
I lay on earth tide-flung, obtruding
Miles of heart and mind, an alien hulk
Into a thumb assemblage. My feet
Were scaled as mountains. Fearful I was
Lest, rising, I dislodge a crossbeam
Of their skies. And this was well, I
Proved obedient to their laws: alien minds
Must learn recumbent postures. A brief
Impulse to unguided knowledge raised
A shower of needles, full-fanged, venom-bodied
I took their meaning, pressed my hands
To earth. They quenched my fleshly thirst
In draughts of Lethe, and I was plunged
Deep in mindless trance. Wheels approached,
They bore me through the famished blades –
As dead the living come into necropolis –
Corded to a span of tumbrils, drugged.

They lodged me in a hall of sorts
A desecrated temple – and this proved sign
Of much that came to pass. I schooled me
In their ways, picked a wary course
Through egg-shell structures. I looked above
Their draughty towers, peered within
Secret chambers, and marvelled at their councils.
Peacock vain, mannikin cruel, sycophant.

The world was measured to a dwarf
Sufficiency; the sun by state decree
Was lowered to fit the sextant of their mind
And planets sighted lower to turn
In calculable grooves, in orbits centred
On the palace of the Sun of suns,
Man-Mountain, King of Lilliput, Lord
And Terror of a thimble universe!

In such surrounds, in truth of fire
Was it a wonder I would sagely err?
How could a stranger tell an earthly sun
Identify as meteors matchwood tongues
Licking lawns, toy orchards, fairy groves?
In plainsight I decried an earthly burn
And squelched the puny flames in fountains
Of urine.

I sought nor favour nor reward, content
In civic duty done, presence of mind
Quick thinking. Alas! This act was rain
Upon long stunted passions,
Customs, taboos, parched sensibilities;
The storm unleashed within the chamberpot
Was long subsiding. Time passed. I kissed
The Queen's fingers. The land bestowed
A Royal Pardon. I pledged my strength anew
To service of the state, enticed the court
Statesmen, minions and nobility
To grace my temple home. They trod a measure
On the dais of my handkerchief
The king excelled in skating on a mucus

Rink – indeed we passed the rapid days
In feasts of love, in mirth and mutual service.

The seasons passed of peace, winds gathered
To a storm within an egg-cup.
Excavating scrolls in long forgotten archives
They stretched the warps of mind to rigid poles
Of opposition, blared the martial note:
From Us the Lillywhite King Lillypuss
To you obfuscating Blefuscoons
From Us the Herrenyolk of Egg
To you Albinos of the Albumen.... We Declare ...!

I could not choose but serve
I took their measure in the depth
Of sea-beds, galley-slave to claims
Of bread and salt. I brought the enemy fleet
To port, and pressed a reasoned course
Of temperate victory. It did not suffice.
I pledged reversion of my strength
To arbitration; they pledged extinction of their kind.
At this rebellion of the galley slave
They looked much, said little. I waded
Home in high-tide of their hate.

Indictments flowed at secret sessions
The palace deed re-echoed, concluding –
Imprimis: Unless by aid of Secret Powers
No human bladder could eject such potent
Piss to douse sidereal flames. Thus:
Imprimis: A blasphemer who dared mistake
Cosmic conflagration for mundane disaster, and –
For paradox: An arsonist for dwarfing
Flames of Lilliput with stark reflection.

From a capital doom, the saving thought
Was waste disposal – how rid the state
Of carrion weightier than the court and state.
The Court Hygienists voiced a dread
Of plagues, infections, cautioned – Hold!
A cult of septic hydrants may derive
From such a monumental corpse, springing
To douse orthodoxies of state and power
In rank corrosive draughts! A compromise
Was sought and found, the sentence writ:

The fault is not in ill-will but in seeing ill
The drab-horse labours best with blinkers
We pardon him to lose his sight to a cure
Of heated needles, that proven cure for all
Abnormalities of view – foresight, insight
Second sight and all solecisms of seeing –

Called vision.

ULYSSES

Notes from here to my Joyce class

Haunting the music of the mind, I watched
Once, through sun slats, a raindrop
Lengthen out to rivers on a window-pane
And on this painless rack of time, stretched
I was, heritage of thought, clay and voices
Passing easily to wind and rain-becoming
And, lest I lose the landmarks of my being
Pocked the air with terse, echoing rounds
Drumtap feelers on the growth of leaves.

This storm has cold wings, and they beat
An interchange in time to death and birth
The rain's harrowing passion, midwife love
Winds newcomer-wanderer in its toils.
Lodged in barenness of ante-rooms
To manger-haven, I, sleep-walker through
The weary cycle of the season's womb
Labouring to give birth to her deathless self,
One more reveller at the rites, I watch
The years re-lay their yeasting dregs
Beneath the froth, hard soles travel pressed
In poultice of new loam. We embrace,
The world and I in great infinitudes.
I grow into that portion of the world
Lapping my feet, yet bear the rain of nails
That drill within to the archetypal heart
Of all lone wanderers.

How pleasant to have toyed with concepts.
Time – we touched upon it – Time I hold
Beyond my hands, a febrile heart slowing
To the calm of death. It weighs all and nothing,
Ceased with rain and ran between my fingers.
It was a crystal cover on the world
A rake of thunders showered its fragments
To a slow dissolve in hailstones, and I was
Held awhile to its truthfulness of transience.
But not for long. It flowed to raise a flotsam from
Tobacco shreds, weaving space inflated
To a swell of dancing seas and pygmy fountains –
Detritus of change, warts on continuity
Drowned steeples of the broken sees, tossed thorn
In matriseas – mud consummation. I trail
A sea-weed cord to hold your breaths to mine
Prime turd among a sea of faeces – oh how
We surf-wrestle to manure the land at ebb!
How golden finally is the recovered fleece?
A question we refuse to ask the Bard.

It turns on quest cycles, to track a skein
Of self through eyeless veils, stumble on warps
Endure the blinds of spidery distortions, till
Swine-scented folds and caressing tunnels
Come to crossroads at the straits, between
Vaginal rocks. Here, the moment of time's
Overlap, forfeiture of flesh, we shed
Our questions, here, turn from bridging
Passes of eroded runs, from scratching
Upon the calloused skin of blind redemptive
Doors. On minds grown hoary from the quest

Rest, rooted even in the turmoil agency
A boulder solitude amidst wine-centred waves
And hold, in paradox of lighthouse windows
On dark-fallen seas, our lighted beings
Suspended as mirages on the world's reality.

Chimes of Silence

At first there is a peep-hole on the living.

It sneaks into the yard of lunatics, lifers, violent and violated nerves, cripples, tuberculars, victims of power sadism safely hidden from questions. A little square hole cut in the door, enough for a gaoler's fist to pass through and manipulate the bolt from either side. Enough also for me to – casually, oh so casually – steal a quick look at the rare flash of a hand, a face, a gesture; more often a blur of khaki, the square planted rear of the guard on the other side.

Until one day, a noise of hammering. All morning an assault of blows multiplied and magnified by the unique echoing powers of my crypt. (When it thunders, my skull *is* the anvil of gods.) By noon that breach is sealed. Only the sky is now open, a sky the size of a napkin trapped by tall spikes and broken bottles, but a sky. Vultures perch on a roof just visible from another yard. And crows. Egrets overfly my crypt and bats swarm at sunset. Albino bats, sickly pale, emitting radio pips to prowl the echo chamber. But the world is dead, suddenly. For an eternity after ceasing the hammers sustain their vehemence. Even the sky retracts, dead.

Buried alive? No. Only something men read of. Buoys and landmarks vanish. Slowly, remorselessly, reality dissolves and certitude betrays the mind.

Days weeks months, then as suddenly as that first death, a new sound, a procession. Feet approach, dragging to the clank of chains. And now another breach that has long remained in-different, blank, a floodhole cut in the base of the wall, this emptiness slowly, gracelessly, begins to frame manacled feet. Nothing has ever passed so close, so ponderously across the floodhole of the Wailing Wall. (I named it that, because it overlooks the yard where a voice cried out in agony all of one night and died at dawn, unattended. It is the yard from which hymns and prayers rise with a constancy matched only by the vigil of crows and vultures.) And now, feet. Bare except for two pairs of boots which consciously walk deadweight to match the pace of manacles on the others. Towards noon the same procession passes the other way. Some days later the procession again goes by and I count. Eleven. The third day of this procession wakes into the longest dawn that ever was born and died of silence, a silence replete and awesome. My counting stops brusquely at six. No more. In that instant the ritual is laid bare, the silence, the furtive conspiracy of dawn, the muffled secrets hammer louder than manacles in my head, all all is bared in one paralysing understanding. Five men are walking the other way, five men walking even more slowly, wearily, with the weight of the world on each foot, on each step towards eternity. I hear them pause at every scrap of life, at every beat of the silence, at every mote in the sun, those five for whom the world is about to die.

Sounds. Sounds acquire a fourth dimension in a living crypt. A definition which, as in the case of thunder becomes physically unbearable. In the case of the awaited but unheard, psychically punishing. Pips from albino bats pock the babble of evensong – moslem and christian, pagan and unclassifiable. My crypt they turn into a cauldron, an inverted bell of faiths whose sonorities are gathered, stirred, skimmed, sieved in the warp and weft of sooty mildew on walls, of green velvet fungus woven by the rain's cunning fingers. From beyond the Wall of Mists the perverse piety of women, that inhuman patience to which they are born drifts across to lash the anguish from the Wall of Purgatory. A clap of wings – a white-and-ochre bolt, a wood-pigeon diving and crossing, a restless shuttle threading sun-patches through this darkest of looms. Beyond and above the outside wall, a rustle of leaves – a boy's face! A guileless hunter unmasks, in innocence – an evil labyrinth. I shall know his voice when children's songs invade the cauldron of sounds at twilight, this pulse intrusion in the home of death.

The sun is rising behind him. His head dissolves in the pool, a shuttle sinking in a fiery loom.

BEARINGS

I   WAILING WALL

Wall to polar star, wall of prayers
A roof in blood-rust floats beyond
Stained-glass wounds on wailing walls
Vulture presides in tattered surplice
In schism for collection plates, with –

Crow in white collar, legs
Of toothpick dearth plunged
Deep in a salvaged morsel. Choirmaster
When a hymn is called he conducts,
Baton-beaking their massed discordance:
Invocation to the broken Word
On broken voices

    Air-tramp, black verger
    Descend on dry prayers
    To altars of evil
    And a charity of victims

On your raft of faith, calling
Darkest dawn to nightfall
I fear in vain you exorcise the past
For evil is impenitent, evil feeds
Upon the wounds and tears of piety
O Wall of prayers, preyed upon
By scavenger, undertaker.

Nightly the Plough
Furrows deep in graveyards of the sky
For a mass burial
Before the lowering poised
A long low coffin of the roof
Bulks against the sky –
Glow of mourning candles in far spaces

Cloud drifts across the Plough
The share is sunk, and hope
Buried in soil of darkness.

II   WALL OF MISTS

Wall of mists, wall of echoes
High pitch, shrill laughter
They feed no fires, prompt no pains
Wake no memories: walls
Are the tomb of longing

Witches' Sabbath what you hold
Vermilion lizards in sun orgies
Monster beetles in wall ulcers, broiled
In steam of mildew drying

Mists of metamorphosis
Men to swine, strength to blows
Grace to lizard prances, honour
To sweetmeats on the tongue of vileness

There rose a shrillness in the air
Grunts, squeals, cackles, wheezes

Remainder membranes of once human throats
A thundercrack in air – the whip
Of Circe calling home her flock
Of transformations?

And echoes roam of disembodied laughter
Borne on soiled streams, sound-waves
On maze of underwall gutters
Brown waters, the lost and dispossessed
Flow beneath my feet, flotsam of the living dead
Dark channels, link of all bereaved.

Pale bats at twilight
Rank incense to efface the sun
A dark of shifting shadows
Vapours of the purple paste
Of sunset.

III   AMBER WALL

Breath of the sun, crowned
In green crepes and amber beads
Children's voices at the door of Orient

Raising eyelids on the sluggish earth
Dispersing sulphur fumes above the lake
Of awakening, you come hunting with the sun

His hands upon the loftiest branches
Halted on the prize, eyes in wonderlust
Questioned this mystery of man's isolation

Fantasies richer than burning mangoes
Flickered through his royal mind, an open
Noon above the door that closed

I would you may discover, mid-morning
To the man's estate, with lesser pain
The wall of gain within the outer loss

Your flutes at evening, your seed-awakening
Dances fill the night with growth; I hear
The sun's sad chorus to your starlit songs

IV   PURGATORY

Wall of flagellation to the South
Strokes of justice slice a festive air –
It is the day of reckoning

In puppet cast: first, by law compelled
The surgeon, ether primed for the ordeal
Next, a cardboard row of gaolers, eyelids
Of glue – the observation squad. And:
Hero of the piece, a towering shade across
The prostrate villain, cuts a trial swathe
In air, nostalgic for the thumbscrew
Rack and nail extractors – alas, all
Good things shall pass away – he adapts
To the regulation cane. Stage props:
Bench for a naked body, crusted towel,

Pail of antiseptic yellow to impart
Wet timbres to dry measures of the Law.

　　The circus comes to circus town
　　A freak show comes to freaks
　　An ancient pageant to divert
　　Archetypes of Purgatorio

For here the mad commingle with the damned.
Epileptics, seers and visionaries
Addicts of unknown addictions, soulmates
To the vegetable soul, and grey
Companions to the ghosts of landmarks
Trudging the lifelong road to a dread
Judicial sentence

And some have walked to the edge of the valley
Of the shadow; and, at a faint stir in memories
Long faded to the moment of the miracle of reprieve
To a knowledge of rebirth and a promise of
tomorrows
And tomorrows and an ever beginning of tomorrows
The mind retreats behind a calloused shelter
Of walls, self-censor on the freedom of remembrance
Tempering visions to opaque masonry, to rings
Of iron spikes, a peace of refuge passionless
And comfort of a gelded sanity.

Weaned from the moment of death, the miracle
Dulled, their minds dissolve in vagueness, a look
Empty as all thoughts are featureless which
Plunge to that lone abyss – And
Had it there ended? Had it all ended, there
Even in the valley of the shadow of Night?

I

Corpse of Vault Centre and the lone
Wood-pigeons breast my ghostly thoughts
On swelling prows of down, plunge
To grass-roots, soar to fountains of the sun

League of sun-gleaners, coursers
On golden chutes, air-gliders feather-vain
On wind-currents, you have fed –
Richer than ravens bald Elijah,

With arcs and eights, death-dives
And love-duets, frilled parabolas
Curved beams and vaulting on my air-ceiling –
This still centre of our compass points.

II

A choir of egrets, servers at the day's
Recessional, on aisles fading to the infinite

Standard bearers of twilight, pride
Of sky-order, coasting homeward with the sun

Bearing vespers from the wall of prayers
To gods unknown, altar-cloths of dusk

Host of communion wafers to dissolve
Within the closing lips of day

My quiver empties to the eternal quest
A needle's glimmer in the emptiness of night
The day's sift filters down
And I, a shawl of grey repose
Fine moves of air, gather dusks in me
An oriel window, eye on chapel ruins.

PROCESSION

Hanging day. A hollow earth
Echoes footsteps of the grave procession
Walls in sunspots
Lean to shadows of the shortening morn

Behind, an eyepatch lushly blue.
The wall of prayer has taken refuge
In a peace of blindness, closed
Its grey recessive deeps. Fretful limbs

And glances that would sometimes
Conjure up a drawbridge
Raised but never lowered between
Their gathering and my sway

Withdraw, as all the living world
Belie their absence in a feel of eyes
Barred and secret in the empty home
Of shuttered windows. I know the heart
Has journeyed far from present

Tread. Drop. Dread Drop. Dead

What may I tell you? What reveal?
I who before them peered unseen
Who stood one-legged on the untrodden
Verge – lest I should not return.

That I received them? That I
Wheeled above and flew beneath them
And brought them on their way

And came to mine, even to the edge
Of the unspeakable encirclement?
What may I tell you of the five
Bell-ringers on the ropes to chimes
Of silence?
What tell you of rigors of the law?
From watchtowers on stunted walls,
Raised to stay a siege of darkness
What whisper to their football thunders
Vanishing to shrouds of sunlight?

Let no man speak of justice, guilt.
Far away, blood-stained in their
Tens of thousands, hands that damned
These wretches to the pit triumph
But here, alone the solitary deed.

II

Passage. Earth is rich in rottenness of things
A soothing tang of compost filters
Through yeasting seeds, rain-sodden
And festive fermentation, a sweetness
Velvety as mead and maggots

Shade your sight from glare
Of leavings on the mound. The feast is done.
A coil of cigarette ribbon recreates
A violet question on the refuse heap
A headless serpent arched in fire
In vibrancy of tinsel light, winding
To futile answers, barren knowledge.

Passage. A finite step is turned
Aside to spare a bean-cake hive, swarm
Of ant-foragers – do not these
Hold a vital motion of earth?
Grooves in bean-cake scored
With indentations of the carious greed
Of priesthood – how well we know them –
Inheritors of the stricken hearth.

Their hands are closed on emptiness
And opening, shall give nothing out.
Cast your eyes from leavings on the mound
Moulting in the sun, from loosened teeth whose harvest
Plagues the world in serpents.

Passage. A streak of earth on whitewashed stones –
Ghosts. Here old women spat their frail
Sibilant juice, and time was essence
Of the bitter nut seeping from withered gums.
We took their love. Through intertwine
Of owlish fingers on the loom, they gave
And wove a spell against this hour
And kept a vigil upon dearth and death.

The feast is done. See where they pass
Our old women of the loom, and they bring
On silent feet echoes in moult of earth
Indigo shawls filled with burrs of night
We lean forward to a drift of dirges
Reconciled in song to passing over
Across the mortar of fire. A pool
Hanging on the mortar's underside
Stays the folded shuttle of the loom.

Passage. Straits of mildew narrowing
To a doorless barrier of light
This is the last we shall revisit
Passageways of childhood, through rows
Of broadlooms weaving emerald tapestries
To wind the effigy of changing seasons
To move again in quest of fear,

Recall the leathern dark of bats – that
Was shadow of ill they said. Did we pass under?
By day it hung a deathness over all
It froze the sunlight in the flight
Of weavers' hands, lowering portents
In shadow humps, pressing from fig branches.

If you pass under, trap a sky-soul bird
Your foot upon its shadow as it flies.

In the passage of looms, to a hum
Of water rising in dark wells
There to play at trap-the-shuttle
To step on the flight of its shadow-soul
And hold it captive in a home
Of air and threadwaves, a lamp
Of dye-fuels hissing in the sun
Elusive as the thread's design.

By footfall on the shade of wings
On earth, a bird may drop as rain.

Ghost fires, loom whispers, indigo lines
On the broad palm of the loom
Web of air-roots falling into silence

Watching the bird that drops as rain
By a hermit's footfall on the wings

Tread Drop Dread Drop Dead

Spiralled on the unseen beam
Pall-bearer to hereafter, I attend.
Mine the bedraggled wings
Raising a wind's lament to every step
Floating on lakes to cries of drowning
Where pebbles bask in twilights of departing,
Mellowed by the sun's last whispers.

Waiting for a sound that never comes
To footfalls long receded, echoing
In craters newly opened into space
Listening to a falter of feet
Upon the dark threshold.

LAST TURNING

the last among the five

This is the last turning of the road
Around this rockface, self
Encounters self, turn pilgrim now
Into souls' kingdom

This is the last turning of the road
Nature's time-passing tales have gathered
Puns, fables, riddles of the lone
In your passage embodied

Bronzed in seasons of your journeying
Guarded by storms, lulled in earthquake
Pathways narrow on the mountain-top
A sheath for the wanderer

Fingers of thorn on stony hill
Passionate gleaner, a path of weeds
Comes to time's orchard – on beds of vines
Press lenten hands

Shaded by wings of silence, dark
Tapestries of time's unfading imprints
Where the peaks' fine needles have embossed
Missals on the heart

Read therein the earth in tremor
Pierce the day's elusive blindfold
Drink clear-headed of the Night's
Enlightening potion

Whose feet wear companion blisters
To the weathered face of cliffs
Whose night-webbed hands have closed upon
Death's awesome silence

And your companion dead, fallen
On hillside, all were steps on the ascent
Parts to the sum of seekers' questions
Sandals on milestones

Linked by drops shared in evil
To a chrysalis of cairns shall come
Rain's awakening, to heirs of sandals
Waters of insight

Into this last turning, pilgrim
Turn alone and bid you welcome
Into this last kingdom, king
Priest, and subject.

RECESSION *(Mahapralaya*)*

welcome o black dawn
whirl-winged, coeval chimes
marsh-glow of origin, dark
of night's ingestion, welcome
union of flame and seal

into the backward reel of time
the heartwood-proud towers, sinking
have folded down their palanquins
the bowers are indrawn
to the forgotten seed

i woke to bells of dreaded nuptials
to a rumble of wheels in baptismal fonts
a song of cyclones in silence of shells
the dew departing to primacy of waters

i woke egret-breasted to a peace of fire
to a shudder of earth in cavalcades of dawn
blinded at last in a rouse of ashes
i move to a dark of insight – it is time

a carillon of wings in shuttered steeples
ropes to communion bells descend to roots
toll for the last dawn, sink spire, sink light
to ancestry of seed, to the dark-in-being

---

* In Hindu Metaphysics, the return of the universe to its
womb; here, expressed as the consoling experience of man in
the moment of death, the freeing of his being from the
death of the world.

the stems of springs are broken, the unplaced source
turned from fountains and watering of growth
folded to the long sleep of waters, brides on a bed of germ
in the unbroken seed

cliffs of clay have walled the human pass
a lifelong fall of ash has sealed the straits
now flares the savaged ember
now lifts the pinioned egret through the pass

breasting the backward drift of hours
the heights are parted to the stress of wings
and his the final argosy, white courier
free, the impenetrable moiety

homing to purify space of measure
lodestone of star courses, turning
belts on the home voyage of planets
navel of apocalyptic tides. . . .

a spring is touched by appointed fingers

and whirlwings fold into the dark
a glacier mind of all-being
slows to a last enduring thought
a deadweight seal of silence sways
upon the secret – at this wake

none keeps vigil. none.

HUNT OF THE STONE*

interlude for the meteor that plunged earthwards months later, and fell – within the hanging yard?

Where lightning heads collide, and
A blot of darkness breaks and traces
Landscapes of the banished heart, there
Too instant for the rain's reflecting lakes
A form is poised, and folding
Sinks to a labyrinth of doubts

To a lure of thunderstones mortal ears
Are tuned, seeking, they know not why
Except as lodestones point to meeting-place
They turn to poles of space.

And a garbage heap may hold, sealed
In tunnel of its fiery violation
A primeval shrine, a searing run
In chambers of immortal silence

As dark unholy surfeits
Shape the clean ascetic silo
Long travelled in dimensions of the loom
The bird of pressed wings may come to rest

---

* When lightning strikes the priests of Sango god of thunder
hunt for the stone and take possession of the goods of the
stricken house, doubly impoverishing the unfortunate
inmates. There is a myth also that Sango strikes down
malefactors or their homes. In whatever case the priests
profit, first by the magical resources of the 'stone' and then
by the forfeited goods.

The tapestry of cycles, rolled
And hoarded to a chosen germ
Within the silent sentinel, may wake
To lonely chimes of rain

Thrust from a spyhole writhes
The unleavened agent, dumb and blinded,
The stone has taken vengeance on the dare
Of perjured eyes, and he was balked
Razed and shattered, bared
To the awesome rhapsody of light.

Priest and acolyte, swinge of incense
At the barrier of immanence –
Homage of clay hearts. Frail
Their fingers tend the weaker flame
But they hover, full of evil rites
To trap the frozen lake of distant fires
In walls of hate and terror.

Ants in their own teeth grooving
They scurry, their hands
Closing ever upon emptiness

They cast their ring of spells around
The ruined hermitage of the Visitation
In a bed of ash, sheltered in lowly beams
Hidden from world-weal and death depression
A nestling glow, the slumbering centre
Of the universe

They asked this hermit but he would not know
His outer blindness looked within their guise

His foot was gentle on the flow of wings
Waiting, peaceful in passage of the looms.

A gleam among the rubble, a coral eye
Watchful on passage. Priest-scavengers
All shall lose their way, their hands
Shall close on emptiness, even their cunning
Fingers of brass. They shall hold
Nought but husks of the seed of passage, though
They sift in ashes of eternity. The shuttle-eel
Shall their nets escape though they cast
In waters of the Deluge.

SPACE

His mind was boundless when out
He flew, he was a true-cast silence
On air and water manifold
Thrust from the matrix of an ark

Breath of light, weaver-wings in loom
Of the immeasurable, from cusp
Of praying hands parted to redeem
Pledges of the first, unbroken Fiat

He flies to test the deluge for a straw
Fording the shrouded estuary of wrath
Courier from caulk and roof of the favoured
Flotsam, one among the perished all

Through webs of fireflies he drove
A gentle wedge in sapwood of the sky
As true as pilgrim comes to springs
Homed the white shadow on the loom

His plenitude a white tent laid
On cobalt sands, and he, forecourser –
Lest the flood cycles be forgot –
Plucks the caravan a date. The stone
The heartstone source of true mirages
Opens to a fiery oasis on the East

Wingless it flew, incense-boat inlaid
With currents of hope, a quiver of mist
Dipping to a bodiless song of air
An oval robe of moonlight paling
A period luminous with silence, drawn
To ghost fingers on the enamoured loom

Between the outward journey and the glance
Backward to a glaze of surfaces before
Untenanted, he saw – newsprung
Dust interstices to measure space!

Is it a wonder he will not return?
He seeks his rest on crosswinds
Emptying to one inchoate flux
Eternal deluge of a Word's design!

SEED

Roll away the stone to echoes
Of silver reins retreating. Wash ears
Of corn in rain to await dawn's embassy
Unshroud the cavern's other mouth
Where Lazarus sheds his rags and tears.

Hour of kernel-baiting
Hour of wrestling dreams awake
Splitting wood-grains to reveal
The hoard of time from passages of fear
Seeking womb-fruit lest it sink again
In tepid ash.

Light the old hearths
With salt and oil, with tubers
Camwood, chalk and antimony
What will they tell us, these
Dark ancestors of the doom?

I speak in the voice of gentle rain
In whispers of growth
In sleight of light
I speak in aged hairs of wind
Midwife to cloud
And sheaves on threshing-floor

I speak in the tread of waters
In fingers of thatch
In veined palm of the unseen guest
Pressing on roof for admittance

I wait on the winnowing run
Of breezes, on songs gathered
To green ears in a field of sap
I wait on footpads of the rain

I waited on the sonorous sift
Of ashes, and I was plucked
As tendril strings by questers' fingers
Rhymed to notations of ebony rings

I fold as rings
Falling from silence of petrified years
To animystic moments of all sleep
Counted in grains of sand or wood
Into whose perfumed bosom we shall drop

As heavy worlds, gather
As grains in full-sap weaving of the field
To winds of passage

Drop, as moments, dissolve
In solitudes of dark ebony essence
Dirge, loom, emptiness of passage.

Prisonnettes

The form was quite arbitrary, something short enough and as self-containing as possible to remain in the head until, at night-time or in a slack moment of surveillance I could transfer it to the inside of a cigarette packet or an equally precious scrap of salvage. The verses naturally belong to several groups, perhaps the only two that require comment being (1) the 'cursifying' or letting-out-rage genre, of whose efficacy let no man stand in doubt, and (2) the so-called Animystic spells which induced a state of self-hypnosis (by constant repetition, accompanied by a mental pacing of the images), an attempt so to speak, to hold and follow through such images in the mind as the words are muttered). The result – a state of weightlessness etc. etc. familiar enough to those who dabble in the more esoteric religions. Both acted as counter to each other: in such situations it is easy to be self-destructively violent (internally) as to be self-destructively quiescent and forgiving.

The prisonnettes are dedicated to all who participated in the two-year experiment on how to break down the human mind. (Including of course those who gave the orders.)

LIVE BURIAL

Sixteen paces
By twenty-three. They hold
Siege against humanity
And Truth
Employing time to drill through to his sanity

Schismatic
Lover of Antigone!
You will? You will unearth
Corpses of yester-
Year? Expose manure of present birth?

Seal him live
In that same necropolis.
May his ghost mistress
Point the classic
Route to Outsiders' Stygian Mysteries.

Bulletin:
He sleeps well, eats
Well. His doctors note
No damage
Our plastic surgeons tend his public image.

Confession
Fiction? Is truth not essence
Of Art, and fiction Art?
Lest it rust
We kindly borrowed his poetic licence.

Galileo
We hoped he'd prove – age
Or genius may recant – our butchers
Tired of waiting
Ordered; take the scapegoat, drop the sage.

Guards The lizard:
Every minute scrapes
A concrete mixer throat.
The cola slime
Flies to blotch the walls in patterned grime

The ghoul:
Flushed from hanging, sniffles
Snuff, to clear his head of
Sins – the law
Declared – that morning's gallows load were dead of.

The voyeur:
Times his sly patrol
For the hour upon the throne
I think he thrills
To hear the Muse's constipated groan

FLOWERS FOR MY LAND

From a distant
Shore they cry, Where
Are all the flowers gone?
I cannot tell
The gardens here are furrowed still and bare.

Death alike
We sow. Each novel horror
Whets inhuman appetites
I do not
Dare to think these bones will bloom tomorrow

Garlands
Of scavengers weigh
Heavy on human breasts
Such
Are flowers that fill the garden of decay

Seeking:
Voices of rain in sunshine
Blue kites on ivory-cloud
Towers
Smell of passing hands on mountain flowers

I saw:
Four steel kites, riders
On shrouded towers
Do you think
Their arms are spread to scatter mountain flowers?

Seeking: Truth
Seeds split and browse

In ordure, corruption. From
Beds of worms
Ivory towers uphold the charnel-house

I know
Of flowers unseen, and they
Distil beatific dawns
But tares
Withhold possession of our mangled lawns

Visions pall
Realities invade
Our innermost sanctuaries
Oil erupts
Upon the altar, casts an evil shade

Hooded hands
Knock upon our doors
We say, let them have place
And offer
Ours in hope to make a common cause

It cannot be!
Hands of slag, fingers
Of spike, they press to full
Possession.
Creepers, climbers thrive beneath their rule

Slogans
Louder than empty barrels
And more barren, a rattle
In cups of beggary
Monkeys in livery dance to barrel organs

Break who can
The yet encroaching ring
Their hands are tainted, their breath
Withers all
They feed their thoughts upon the bounty of death

I traced
A dew-lane on the sun-
flower leaf; a hailstone
Burning, blew
A trap-door on my lane for falling through

These buds
That burst upon our prayers
Diffuse an equal essence
Will for ill
As others their atomic efflorescence

Alienates
Of heart from land, outcasts
Of toadstool blooms, the coral
Is a grim
Historic flower, a now and future moral

Come, let us
With that mangled kind
Make pact, no less
Against the lesser
Leagues of death, and mutilators of the mind.

Take Justice
In your hands who can
Or dare. Insensate sword
Of Power
Outherods Herod and the law's outlawed

Sun-beacons
On every darkened shore
Orphans of the world
Ignite! Draw
Your fuel of pain from earth's sated core.

ANIMYSTIC SPELLS

I

First you must
Walk among the faceless
Their feet are shod in earth
And dung
Caryatids in anterooms of night's inbirth

Shards strewn
On secret passages of night
Their creviced skin is dew
Inlaid, star-wells
For nights of drought, for dearth of light

Hold
As they, bread as breath
Is held and spent, discarding
Weights of time
In clutching and possessing – yokes of death.

The quest
Is all, endless
The home-coming
Respite
Before the gathering of the outward crest

II

Eyes
That grow as stamens need
A yeast of pollen. Shun
Visions
Of the unleavened, look sooner on the sun.

III

Death
Embraces you and I
A twilight cone is
Meeting-place
The silent junction of the grey abyss

IV

The past
Dissolves in lacquered notes
Lips on woodwind, ears
Of grain
Swaying to echoes in a veil of rust

V

Incense
Of pines when a page
Is turned, woodsmoke
Rings
Across a thousand years to a bygone sage

VI

Fragments
We cannot hold, linger
Parings of intuition
Footsteps
Passing and re-passing the door of recognition

VII

Line
Of the withered bough
Hill and broken valleys

Dearth
On thirsty palm to furrows of the earth

VIII

Blood
When it is done – dearth
Of lines from palm to love
Light,
Springs, to patient wrinkles of the earth

IX

Links
Of dust, Whitened rib
Of ghosts to flute
Home-coming
Moth-fingers hover on the new-laid crib

X

Old moons
Set your crescent eyes
On bridges of my hands
Comb out
Manes of sea-wind on my tide-swept sands

XI

Seed:
A bowl of dark unblemish
A chancel closed in forest
Silences
Repletion for earth's own regenerate need

A wind's
Dark mantle brushes past
A quiet prelude to the stir
Of germ
A cycle's ether sieve for pollen hair

Fall seeds
Then, to mineral hands
Flush out in your green
And gentle blades
Awaken minds and grow to cosmic shades

XII

Buried lakes:
My feet, satanic cleft
Spring-divining feet have mined
Buried lakes
Calms in opal caverns of the mind

Incense-boat
Amber flare, a broken
Bolt awash in indigo
Sky and voice
Peace of light before the death token

Sough of wings
Moonsward on night, guides
To skyscapes of the mind
Unfettered
Now begins the flight on memory tides

XIII

Offerings
That cling to us teach
To give is to suffer
To share
A bitter foretaste of the death we bear

Altar-vessel
Of one skull shall bear
Offerings for the ascent
Multitudes
Shall dance on flesh remains of a cosmic dare

XIV

Three millet
Stalks. A tasselled crown
On a broken glass horizon
Weeds clogged
Their feet, winds came and blew them down

New ears arose
Lean lances through
A stubbed and mangled mound –
And this I saw –
Their grains were ripened closer to the ground.

BACKGROUND AND FRIEZES

They varied Death
A thousand ways – sudden
To piecemeal. Virgins bled
At lepers' orgies
The streets were cobbled with unnumbered dead

Jacques d'Odan
Wise angel not to rush
Where no hero treads
Whispers – stop!
This spree is getting out of hand – and heads

Rinses
Clean fingers in a bowl
Of blood, and humbly adds
Pips and crowns
To a General make-weight of his shoulder-pads

My word
Is bond. Whom I treat
To the sworn safe-conduct
I guarantee
Will journey safely down the one-way street

Street singers
Chant my tune: I am
God's chosen instrument
Do I hear –
Played upon by fat unholy fingers?

Boots? Butts?
Only a mild reproach

He lives, a mud reptilian
Heed sirens!
Drive into the sea at my approach!

Humane
My code of conduct, creed
Of good intentions, gun-mate
Cromwellian style
Some day we'll teach the soldiery to read

Hands off!
My affair's internal
Await my beggar's cup
For when I'm sated
Me to burn, you to grant full aid eternal

A beach
Hides the pebble. Create –
But bleach (or whitewash) –
Cairns
Of bones to hide the skeleton of hate

Futile shield
Before the festive slayers
Mother to child, prayers
Unavailing
The scene is old, cue in the waiting players

Week Seventy-five:
Observers welcome. Cheap
Conducted tours – behold!
Our hands are clean.
The rains have fallen twice and earth is deep.

FUTURE PLANS

The meeting is called
To odium: Forgers, framers
Fabricators Inter-
national. Chairman,
A dark horse, a circus nag turned blinkered sprinter

Mach Three
We rate him – one for the Knife
Two for 'iavelli, Three –
Breaking speed
Of the truth barrier by a swooping detention decree

Projects in view:
Mao Tse Tung in league
With Chiang Kai. Nkrumah
Makes a secret
Pact with Verwoerd, sworn by Hastings Banda.

Proven: Arafat
In flagrante cum
Golda Meir. Castro drunk
With Richard Nixon
Contraceptives stacked beneath the papal bunk . . .

. . . and more to come

Poems of Bread and Earth

RELIEF

Or, Wedding in a Minor Key

Bread is magic, grace.
Some touch the whitefluff only
With crested silver spoon
With coat of arms
And liveried service. Delicately.
Bread is magic, grace. *Your* grace
Is not the pulse of life,
Your Grace.

Bread is magic, grace.
The mouldy crust alone was life and pulse
Dungbread, blackbread, wholebread, rankbread
Sparebreadstockbreadgutbreadbloodandsweatbread –
BREAD!!! was that the victims craved
Locked so long with hate and fear
And fire before their eyes.

When he had
Dined and wined and – surely – wived. . . .
And much human dough there was
Broken round his board and court
Around his state and splendour. . . .
When he had
Dined and wined, and strutted wiving-poised
He ordered:

Empty that plane
Of bread, damn bread! Turn its nose
To a different wind, to a perfumed wind
Fill the hold with cake and wine
And champagne guests – It's time
For MY wedding. And –
Shut those hungry mouths! – I have
Good Precedent.

CAPITAL

It cannot be
That germ which earth has nurtured
Man tended – once I watched a waterfall
Of germ, a grain-spray plenitude
Belched from chutes of wide-mouthed
Glad satiation; I swear the grains
Were singing –

It cannot be
That policy, deliberation
Turns these embers of my life
To ashes, and in polluted seas
Lay sad beds of yeast to raise
Dough
On the world market.

UJAMAA

(for Julius Nyerere)

Sweat is leaven for the earth
Not tribute. Earth replete
Seeks no homage from the toil of earth.
Sweat is leaven for the earth
Not driven homage to a fortressed god.
Your black earth hands unchain
Hope from death messengers, from
In-bred dogmanoids that prove
Grimmer than the Grim Reaper, insatiate
Predators on humanity, their fodder.
Sweat is leaven, bread, Ujamaa
Bread of the earth, by the earth
For the earth. Earth is all people.

EVER-READY BANK ACCOUNTS

Ever-ready bank accounts
Are ever red
Cash may be set on paper, all it reads
Is – Bread Bread Bread! Among a thousand fingers
Clutching loud at plenty, arms
Stacked too full of loaves cannot
Embrace mankind.

Ever-ready bank accounts
Are never read where
Children slay the cockroach for a meal
Awaiting father-forager's return
The mind of hungered innocence must turn
To strange cuisine – kebab of houseflies
On a broomstick prong; beetles broiled in carapace
Slugs are scientific stores of high protein –
They tell me – I never tried it yet.
Awaiting father-forager's return with empty sack
He went and came that way these two-year gone
He will tomorrow . . .
                    I take the folded statement
Slipped below the grill. Discreetly. Below the solemn
Chiding glare of my good friend and foe .
The bank clerk, the white-shirt guardian of the vaults
Of paper, mystic signs, those noughts and crosses
Which I bear – the language of his statement reads:
Charity may be a one-way street, it's not
A one-man way of life. And like the ink
It's printed on, I go red beneath

My black deceit, my bold and knowing
'Damn-they're-late-again-with-that-cheque skin –
You know, my royalties, late again I see
It's alright really, do present it at month's end'
Cursing the last extortion I was guilty of
For falling prey to. I have observed it –
The latest cup of supplicating hands is always
Drier than the last. And rats are sleeker now
Whose raw-eyed thrusts dispute
Crumbs with new-hatched mouths of want. . . .

Now that was long ago, and yesterday, and Now
The longer statement trails a longer line
Of bread, and now again that mournful statement
Marred by sceptic stares – but HE we know,
He earns the sky, commands a fortune when he farts.
And all it reads is that one line, one ledgered statement –
Charity may be a one-way street, it's not
A one-man way of life – Your balance sir
Your balance is that figure etched in red. . . .

A page, a ready reddening reckoner falls open on
The seven-year lease on seven-floor heights
Of the seventh wonder of a pocket world
The seventh wonder of the seven-year plan of lies
Seven times grander than the last grandiose deceit.

Justify the seven-year lease on seven-floor heights:
'I'd live there if I could. I built that
Seven-tiered modest monster for a home
But duties of the seven-year plan demand
My absence thence, and how may seven-year seeds
Not yield a modest sevenfold green return?'

A balance sheet is waved, a flag on stolen heights
And who goes red invisibly beneath their black deceit?
A balance sheet is hung in rags on barren trees
And who turns red invisibly beneath their black despair?
And who turns red for who turns red, and who turns
    when

To light, across that broken road a fire that heals
From logs whose weight upon a great
Grandmother arched in pain still shapes –
A loaded question mark?

APRES LA GUERRE

Do not cover up the scars
In the quick distillery of blood
I have smelt
Seepage from familiar opiates,
Do not cover up the scars

The tuber of our common flesh, when
Trampled deep in earth embattles
Death, new-girthed, lunges at the sun
But lest it prove a hollowed shell
And lest the feet of new-born lives
Sink in voids of counterfeiting
Do not swell earth's broken skin
To glaze the fissures in the drum

Do not cover up with scabs
And turn the pain a masquerader's
Broken-tongued lament
Its face a painted mask of veils
Its breath unmoistened by the run of bile
A patchwork heart and death-head grin
To cheat the rigors of
Exorcism.

Paint cracks. Bequeath
The heartwood beat alone
To new-born
Followers of the wake.

JOURNEY

I never feel I have arrived, though I come
To journey's end. I took the road
That loses crest to questions, yet bears me
Down the other homeward earth. I know
My flesh is nibbled clean, lost
To fretful fish among the rusted hulls –
I passed them on my way

And so with bread and wine
I lack the sharing with defeat and dearth
I passed them on my way.

I never feel I have arrived
Though love and welcome snare me home
Usurpers hand my cup at every
Feast a last supper

Epilogue

AND WHAT OF IT IF THUS HE DIED?

for Victor Banjo
And for George Jackson
And All, All, All

Not that he loved sunrise less
But truly, as love's caress
Whose craving must to spring devices lead.

Nor deaf nor blind lived he
To beauty's promise, to laughter
In light hours, but these he sought
To seal and to perpetuate
Upon the face of dearth.

Knowledge was not a golden plate
For feasts at the board of privilege
But a trowel laid to deep foundations
In sighted fingers of a master mason.

They said unto him, Be still
While winds of terror tore out shutters
Of his neighbour's home.

Beyond their walls to insulate
He felt his eyelids shrivel
In fires of rapine. The wrongs of day
And cries of night burnt red fissures
In chambers of his mind.

And so he set upon the quest
Seeking that whose plenitude
Would answer calls of hate and terror.

He looked with longing
To the lay of ocean pastures
Sought to harness their unbidden depths,

To measure the wind for symmetry
And on the wheel of earth to place
A compass for bewildered minds

He wondered in a treasure-house
Of inward prizes, strove to bring
Fleeting messages of time
To tall expressions, to granite arches
Spanned across landslides of the past

Even in the blind spoliation, amidst
Even the harrying of flames, he wished
To regulate the turn of hours

He lit the torch to a summons
Of the great procession – and, what of it?
What of it if thus he died
Burnt offering on the altar of fears?

FOR CHRISTOPHER OKIGBO

Perhaps 'tis kinder that vultures toil
To cleanse torch-bearers for the soil

Than eagles bare their living bone
Chained to an eternity of stone

Kinder that dying eyes should close
To truths of light on weed and rose

Than read in their own live entrails
Fulfilments of the web of nails

Kinder indeed full reckoning paid
A circle closed, a lowered shade

Leaving their world as blank a slate
As eyelids on the wall of Fate

Kinder that, lured by cleansing rites
He fell, burnt offering on the heights

His torch to waken mountain shrines
Fused to an alien tuber of mines

Yet kinder this, than a spirit seared
In violated visions and truths immured

Eternal provender for Time
Whose wings his boundless thoughts would climb.

*Mandela's
Earth*

—

Mandela's Earth

YOUR LOGIC FRIGHTENS ME, MANDELA

Your logic frightens me, Mandela
Your logic frightens me. Those years
Of dreams, of time accelerated in
Visionary hopes, of savouring the task anew,
The call, the tempo primed
To burst in supernovae round a 'brave new world'!
Then stillness. Silence. The world closes round
Your sole reality; the rest is . . . dreams?

Your logic frightens me.
How coldly you disdain legerdemains!
'Open Sesame' and – two decades' rust on hinges
Peels at the touch of a conjurer's wand?
White magic, ivory-topped black magic wand,
One moment wand, one moment riot club
Electric cattle prod and whip or *sjambok*
Tearing flesh and spilling blood and brain?

This bag of tricks, whose silk streamers
Turn knotted cords to crush dark temples?
A rabbit punch sneaked beneath the rabbit?
Doves metamorphosed in milk-white talons?
Not for you the olive branch that sprouts
Gun muzzles, barbed-wire garlands, tangled thorns
To wreathe the brows of black, unwilling Christs.

Your patience grows inhuman, Mandela.
Do you grow food? Do you make friends
Of mice and lizards? Measure the growth of grass
For time's unhurried pace?
Are you now the crossword puzzle expert?

Chess? Ah, no! Subversion lurks among
Chess pieces. Structured clash of black and white,
Equal ranged and paced? An equal board? No!
Not on Robben Island. Checkers? Bad to worse.
That game has no respect for class or king-serf
Ordered universe. So, scrabble?

Monopoly? Now, that . . . ! You know
The game's modalities, so do they.
Come collection time, the cards read 'White Only'
In the Community Chest. Like a gambler's coin
Both sides heads or tails, the 'Chance' cards read:
Go to jail. Go straight to jail. Do not pass 'GO'.
Do not collect a hundredth rand. Fishes feast,
I think, on those who sought to by-pass 'GO'
On Robben Island.

Your logic frightens me, Mandela, your logic
Humbles me. Do you tame geckos?
Do grasshoppers break your silences?
Bats' radar pips pinpoint your statuesque
Gaze transcending distances at will?
Do moths break wing
Against a light bulb's fitful glow
That brings no searing illumination?
Your sight shifts from moth to bulb,
Rests on its pulse-glow fluctuations –
Are kin feelings roused by a broken arc
Of tungsten trapped in vacuum?

Your pulse, I know, has slowed with earth's
Phlegmatic turns. I know your blood
Sagely warms and cools with seasons,
Responds to the lightest breeze
Yet scorns to race with winds (or hurricanes)
That threaten change on tortoise pads.

Is our world light-years away, Mandela?
Lost in visions of that dare supreme
Against a dire supremacy of race,
What brings you back to earth? The night guard's
Inhuman tramp? A sodden eye transgressing through
The Judas hole? Tell me Mandela,
That guard, is he *your* prisoner?

Your bounty threatens me, Mandela, that taut
Drumskin of your heart on which our millions
Dance. I fear we latch, fat leeches
On your veins. Our daily imprecisions
Dull keen edges of your will.
Compromises deplete your act's repletion –
Feeding will-voided stomachs of a continent,
What will be left of you, Mandela?

LIKE RUDOLF HESS, THE MAN SAID!

'We keep him (Mandela) for the same reason the Allied Powers are holding Rudolf Hess.'
— Pik Botha, South African Foreign Minister

Got you! Trust the Israelis.
I bet they flushed him out, raced him down
From Auschwitz to Durban, and Robben Island.
Mandela? Mandel . . . Mendel . . . Mengel . . . Mengele!
It's he! Nazi superman in sneaky blackface!

A brilliant touch – let's give the devil his due.
Who would seek the Priest of Vivisections
Masquerading as a Black-and-Proud?
No living heart in mouth, one step ahead
Those Jew-vengeance squads.
Safe on Robben Island, paratroops of Zion
Bounty hunters, frogmen, crack Z squads,
Wiesenthal fanatics – here you'll find
Robben Island is no Entebbe. This pogrom maestro
Has his act together – he'll serve time
To spit on borrowed time!

A cunning touch, those modest body counts
In Sharpeville, Soweto. In your heydays,
The crop was tens of thousands. Now who would once
Surmise the mastermind directing death
In tens? Or twenties? Even hundreds!

In your luxurious island home, outfitted
State-of-the-art laboratory, ideas
Flow out to pay the state in kind – protection

For caste research, food for thought.
The ninety-day detention law – your idea?
A ninety-day laboratory per man.
Blackened cells – not padded, no –
You diagnosed inferior minds, not madness. Cells
So lightproof, even the stereotypic eyes
Shed their white pretence – Black is Beautiful?
You made them taste sublimity in Blacked-Out
Solitary.

You listened to their minds go loudly awry.
Mere operational change, from flaying live;
'Improving' on those naïve tries of nature.
Do you feel nostalgia for the past?
Stripping the 'circumcised dogs' to buff and
Searching secret parts for jewellery? And your love
For gold teeth – ah yes, gold!
Gassed them cold and questioned their anatomy.
Too bad some woke midsurgery,
But you swung the pendulum the other way
And thousands died from greedy inhalation –
They loved the stuff, they died laughing, no?

Gold! They wore their ransom in their teeth
Their dowry, tithes, death duties. But –
No need *here* for that painful dentistry,
Assaying the yellow fire even before
The body is cold. Our Broederland
Flaunts the gold standard of the world.
Black muscles work it – quickly you adjusted –
None but racial slanderers now predict
A genocide. Modestly you shun the Final Solution –
Who slays the goose that lays such golden eggs?

The gold exposed you. Bloodhound Jews
Whose mouth you quarried for your pay –
Your passion tasting still of blood –
Set their burgled gums to track you down
To the golden tip of the black continent.

Cute Mandgela, sought everywhere,
Cooly ensconced on Robben Island.
I saw your hand in Biko's death, that perfect
Medical scenario, tailormade for you.
And hundreds more of young Icarus syndrome –
Flying suspects, self-propelled
From fifty-storey floors
To land on pavements labelled – WHITES ONLY!
You question them only in white preserves –
How would a high-rise building fit in shantytown?

So desperate for acceptance, exhibitionist,
Made omelette of their brains for white
Rights of passage. Sheer sophistry! Skin
Is deep enough. Your lancet Mandgele, was genius,
Creator hand so deft, made anaesthetic
Optional – blue cornea graft, heart-liver swap,
Organic variants – eye in earholes, leg to armpit,
Brain transfer – all child's play to you, but –
Not even you could work a whole-skin graft.
A thousand dead in the attempt
Makes proof enough – wouldn't you say?

Mendgela's in town – the word is passed.
Keep park benches sanitised. White is white
(Though sometimes Jew but – times do change.) –
Black is red is commie menace

Red is what we see when Icarus leaps
A red-forked lightning from cloud-hugging floors,
Tight-lipped, fork-tongued, terror mentors,
Beclouding issues clearly black and white.

And the racial traitors – white Ruth First,
Opens a letter in Harare – *Boom!* – Alibied,
You smile on Robben. Too bad, re coloured Brutus,
Mister *Boots, Knuckles and Bones*. Too athletic?
Caught a bullet but it missed the vital organs
Trying to beat us to the Olympic laurels.
Hassling, hounding Bundbroederland from sports
Our lifeblood, proof of stock and breeding –
Cowards! Like their new uneasy allies –
Those back-stabbing, 'trading partners' –
Scared of competition? Of open contest? Right!
We have the carats; keep your plated medals!

Gold! Ah yes, Mandela-Hess,
You got us in this mess. The Allied Powers
Rightly hold you pacing wall to wall,
Treading out your grand designs
In commie jackboots. Mandela-Mengele,
You are *ours!* We'll keep you close.
Your *Doppelgänger* haunts us to the vaults.
Yes, 'thars gold in them thar mountains' – would *you*
Let Mandela loose?

SO NOW THEY BURN THE
ROOF ABOVE HER HEAD

For Winnie

So now they burn the roof above her head?
Well, what's new? Retarded minds, like infants,
Play with fire. Bright things attract them.
Colour obsessed, did not these mewling agents once
Arrest your bedspread?

       It wore, remember,
The colours of the ANC. The patchwork quilt
Inflamed their eyes, dancing in defiance.
They came, they searched, rampaged as only
Red-flag-baited bulls know how. They found
This sheet of love, but hate pursued them.

'My bed, our spread, our bedspread,'
She protested. 'A quilt,' she taught them,
'By many hands embroidered, it holds
And shares our love, our toil, with all who toil
And share.

'This bedspread knows the pangs of birth.
Like earth in hope of our remaking, it is
Generous in love, a feast
Cast wide to embrace all man and womankind.
Do you wonder then, it wears the hues of hope?

'Love is not lone fulfilled. Embrace
Is gathering-in, the love of man and woman
Leaven in the dough of nation love.

This nest, this rest, this haven from white storms
You raise to thwart homecoming, this battered
Sailcloth mourns the fallen, celebrates
Our rites of passage. Nuptial train and shroud,
Blood stanch or swaddling cloth, desk
And breakfast tray in heat of battle – Foe,
Why marvel it does wear the stripes of strife?

'A standard points the weary feet forward, yet
Wraps the hero's final stillness.
This bedspread cushions us
Against the fall that absence makes.'

Still they took her spread away, Mandela
And now they burn the roof above her head.

Nonperson, outlawed of social being,
'Banned.' Her image whited out in old group photos
(But who can scrub the mind's retentive plates?)
Her name in blanks, her tongue discoloured
By the censor's crayon, they crowed:
'She'll gather mould and time dust, spin
Her censored being in cobwebs of oblivion.'
Midmind lies in history's teeth! She was
The rare illuminated scroll in whose prophesies
Humanity discerns its fate. The world would read her
In a hundred tongues.

Whited sepulchres – it is their nature –
Disgorge forgotten leprosies.
Minds in midform, trapped in medieval shrouds,
Their sickness conjured out

Flames of hell, Inquisition's bonfires.
In Winnie they descried all heresiarchs –
Joan of Arc to Salem Seers – frenzied now,
They piled up faggots for the auto-da-fé.

Mammon's Grand Alliances
Begin to crack. The League of Hypocrites
Read the scroll, traceries of fire provide
The dreaded annotations, turn laser heat
To melt the prison bars.

No wonder then, and thus no need to curse
The futile rage, the puny stabs of flames
Disfiguring the night. Death twitches these
Of centuries' buried minds in midformation.
This Witches' Sabbath they invoke will hone
The wooden stake to drive deep through the heart
Of the living dead.

I know they took the spread away, Mandela
And now they burn the roof above her head.
How could they know, these living dead
The flames their fumbling hands have fanned
Inscribe the very colours they proscribe
Across our darkest nights.

FUNERAL SERMON, SOWETO

We wish to bury our dead. Now, a funeral
Is a many-cultured thing. Some races would
Rope a heifer to the slaughter stone, or
Goat/ram/pig or humble cockerel,
Monochrome or striped, spotted, seamless –
The soothsayer rules the aesthetics or,
Rank and circumstance of the dear deceased.
Market rates may ruin devout intentions.
Times austere are known to sanction disrespect,
Spill thinner blood than wished. Still,
Flow it must. Rank tunnels of transition
Must be greased, the bolt of passage loosened,
Home-brewed beer or smuggler's brands, prestigious,
Froth and slosh with ostentation, belch
In discreet bubbles like embarrassed mourners
At the wake. The dead record no disavowal.

We wish to mourn our dead.
Is custom overlooked? No. Our heads
Are shaven clean. Cropped close. Neglected. Matted
Thick with ritual unguents, spiked with clay
Or fibre. Ceremonials well rehearsed,
All outward acts of group cohesion, smothering
Loss, performed. Our headgears bear clan colours.
Portraits, mementos, icons, elders' mats
Laid out in proud parade, mute debts
Of honour, surrogates to vanished breath.
Mummers, griots, play out lineage roles.
The feats, the voices, reverential anecdotes . . .
All to bind us to the 'dead but not forgotten.'

O dearly beloved, we wish to mourn. But first,
Shall we lance some ancient tumuli? Probe
Some birthly portents, glorified demise?
'When beggars die . . .' You know the verse . . .
But if the heavens launch comets to proclaim
The death of kings, archaeological probes
Catalogue our earthly supplement – spent
Rhetoric of skills our earth hoards yield:
Vaults of coins to bribe the other world,
Inlaid bowls, golden lamps, cryptic stellae,
Astral calculus engraved on marble
Mausoleums – the astrologer's final computation?
The jewelled sword hilt, 'rich beyond all dreams'.
A geography of stasis and cerebral feats
Cheek by jowl across the centuries.
Heliolatrous Incas. Slave and palm oil
Aristocracy on blood-soaked Niger creeks –
Their sportive obsequies arced human skulls,
Fresh-tissued, point to point of silver lances –
Innovative variants of the polo game!
Have we treasures to inter, dear brothers
And sisters? Do we play polo in Soweto?

We wish to bury our dead. Others
Boast horsemen sentinels, ranged in Chinese
Catacombs, silent guards on vanished
Dynasties. Or their Nilotic counterparts –
Did time stand still for these? The labour hours –
Gathering, grading, grinding, mixing,
Mapping the hour of star and moon alignment
To stuff the royal orifice with spices.
Draining toes swelled tuberose with pomp

To ease the slide of rings and golden anklets.
Calf amulets of ivory. Seals on each finger
Equal a nation's ransom. Casque or death mask,
Mines to rival Nature's undiscovered hoards.
Queen, princeling, favourite cat, each
Scrolled in own sarcophagus surround the god-king.
Antechambers lined with lesser beings
Extend the ministry beyond the end
To imagined wants of their lone, lordly dead.

O dearly beloved, seeking solace ever,
Distractions of the mind to ease keen pangs
As we move to bury our dead, we pause only
To contemplate these ancient vanities –
Mongol, Pharaoh, proud Asantehene
All, too lean in frame to fill their grandiose
Subterranean schemes, a troubled sleep
Of ranked retainers swells. Nerveless arms
Redress lost battles, amplify the dream
That thrust a mildewed gauntlet at mortality.
Awesome pyramids on burning sands,
Cunning combs of mind in mountain wombs,
Absentee landlords of necropolis, peopled
By vassals, serfs you dared not leave behind –
How phrased your priests their Final Unction?
Even in death, beware insurrection of life,
And life after debt? Of blood?

We wish to bury our dead. Let all take note,
Our dead were none of these eternal hoarders –
Does the buyer of nothing seek after-sales service?
Not as prophetic intuitions, or sly

Subversive chant do we invoke these ancient
Ghosts, but as that ritual homily
Time-honoured in the offices of loss.
Not seeking martyrdom, the midnight knock,
Desecration of our altar, vestments,
Not courting ninety-day detention laws,
The state seal on the voice of man – and God . . .

We wish only to bury our dead. Shorn
Of all but name, our indelible origin,
For indeed our pride once boasted empires,
Kings and nation builders. Seers. Too soon
The brace of conquest circumscribed our being
Yet found us rooted in that unyielding
Will to life bequeathed from birth, we
Sought no transferred deed of earthly holdings.
Slaves do not possess their kind. Nor do
The truly free.

We wished to bury our dead,
We rendered unto Caesar what was Caesar's.
The right to congregate approved;
Hold procession, eulogise, lament
Procured for a standard fee. All death tariff
Settled in advance, receipted, logged.
A day to cross the barriers of our skin.
Death was accorded purchase rights, a brief licence
Subject to withdrawal – we signed acceptance
On the dotted line – 'orderly conduct' et cetera.
We now proceed to render earth's to earth.

We wish to mourn our dead. No oil tycoons
We, Mandela, no merchant princes, scions
Of titled lineage. No peerage aspirants
Nor tribal chieftains. Only the shirtless
Ghetto rats that briefly left
The cul-de-sac of hunger, stripes,
Contempt. The same that rose on hind legs
That brief hour in Sharpeville, reddening
The sleepy conscience of the world. We,
The sludge of gold and diamond mines,
Half-chewed morsels of canine sentinels
In nervous chain stores, snow-white parks.
Part-crushed tracks of blinded Saracens,
The butt of hippo trucks, water cannon mush.

We, the bulldozed, twisted shapes of
Shanty lots that mimic black humanity.
Our dead bore no kinship to the race
Of lordly dead, sought no companion dead
To a world they never craved.
We set out to mourn our dead, bugling
No Last Post, no boom of guns in vain salute.

But others donned a deeper indigo than the bereaved.
Unscheduled undertakers spat their lethal dirge
And fifty-eight were sudden bright-attired,
Flung to earth in fake paroxysms of grief.
And then we knew them, counted, laid them out,
Companion voyagers to the dead we mourned.

And now, we wish to bury our dead. . . .

'NO!' HE SAID

(for Nelson Mandela)

Shorn of landmarks, glued to a sere promontory,
The breakers sought to crush his head,
To flush the black will of his race
Back in tidal waves, to flesh-trade centuries,
Bile-slick beyond beachcombing, beyond
Salvage operations but – no, he said.

Sea urchins stung his soul. Albino eels
Searched the cortex of his heart,
His hands thrust high to exorcise
Visions of lost years, slow parade of isolation's
Ghosts. Still they came, seducers of a moment's
Slack in thought, but – no, he said.

And they saw his hands were clenched.
Blood oozed from a thousand pores. A lonely
Fisher tensed against the oilcloth of new dawns,
Hand over hand he hauled. The harvest strained.
Cords turned writhing hawsers in his hands. 'Let go!'
The tempters cried, but – no, he said.

Count the passing ships. Whose argosies
Stretch like golden beads on far horizons? Those are
Their present ease, your vanished years. Castaway,
Minnows roost in the hold of that doomed ship
You launched in the eye of storms. Your mast is seaweed
On which pale plankton feed, but – no, he said.

Are you bigger than Nkomati? Blacker
Than hands that signed away a continent for ease?
Lone matador with broken paddle for a lance,
Are you the Horn? The Cape? Sequinned
Constellation of the Bull for tide-tossed
Castaways on pallid sands? No, he said.

The axis of the world has shifted. Even the polar star
Loses its fixity, nudged by man-made planets.
The universe has shrunk. History re-echoes as
We plant new space flags of a master race.
You are the afterburn of our crudest launch.
The stars disown you, but – no, he said.

Your tongue is salt swollen, a mute keel
Upended on the seabed of forgotten time.
The present breeds new tasks, same taskmasters.
On that star planet of our galaxy, code-named Bantustan,
They sieve rare diamonds from moon dust. In choice
    reserves,
Venerably pastured, you . . . but – no, he said.

That ancient largesse on the mountaintop
Shrinks before our gift's munificence, an offer even
Christ, second-come, could not refuse. Be ebony mascot
On the flagship of our space fleet, still
Through every turbulence, spectator of our Brave New
    World.
Come, Ancient Mariner, but – no, he said –

No! I am no prisoner of this rock, this island,
No ash spew on Milky Ways to conquests old or new.
I am this rock, this island. I toiled,

Precedent on this soil, as in the great dark whale
Of time, Black Hole of the galaxy. Its maw
Turns steel-wrought epochs plankton – yes – and
Vomits out new worlds.

In and out of time warp, I am that rock
In the black hole of the sky.

APOLOGIA *(Nkomati*)*

Doyen of walls,
Your puzzled frown has spanned the gulf
Between us.
Your stoic pride rejects, I fear,
This homage paid across four thousand miles,
Unfleshed at source, not manifested
In the act. Justice glowers in your rejection –
I submit:

Utterances flung like lead shot will never
Forge the chain mail of our collective will.
Only the salt of sweat-bathed palms
Pressed in anger will corrode
These prison bars. Our caged eagles
Wait on flight, their sweet-stern cry to stir
Our air again. Our assaulted patience
Waits in concert.

We wear our shame like bells on outcasts.
The snail has feet – I know; our jury
Shuffles to assemblage on the feet of snails.

These retreats in face of need
Betray our being – no wonder
The traitors steep us in contempt!

* The Nkomati Accord: put simply, the nonagression pact
between South Africa and the front-line states.

An old man of sixty-five ekes out his life
In prison slops. The poet
Strings you these lines, Mandela,
To stay from stringing lead.

Deluge and After

AFTER THE DELUGE

Once, for a dare,
He filled his heart-shaped swimming pool
With bank notes, high denomination
And fed a pound of caviar to his dog.
The dog was sick; a chartered plane
Flew in replacement for the Persian rug.

He made a billion yen
Leap from Tokyo to Buenos Aires,
Turn somersaults through Brussels,
New York, Sofia and Johannesburg.
It cracked the bullion market open wide.
Governments fell, coalitions cracked
Insurrection raised its bloody flag
From north to south.

He knew his native land through iron gates,
His sight was radar bowls, his hearing
Electronic beams. For flesh and blood,
Kept company with a brace of Dobermanns.
But – yes – the worthy causes never lacked
His widow's mite, discreetly publicised.

He escaped the lynch days. He survives.
I dreamt I saw him on a village
Water line, a parched land where
Water is a god
That doles its favours by the drop,
And waiting is a way of life.
Rebellion gleamed yet faintly in his eye

Traversing chrome-and-platinum retreats. There,
Hubs of commerce smoothly turn without
His bidding, and cities where he lately roosted
Have forgotten him, the preying bird
Of passage.

They let him live, but not from pity
Or human sufferance. He scratches life
From earth, no worse a mortal man than the rest.
Far, far away in dreamland splendour,
Creepers twine his gates of bronze relief.
The jade-lined pool is home
To snakes and lizards; they hunt and mate
On crusted algae.

APOLLODORUS ON THE NIGER

*– The sale of a continent yet again, in Lagos, during preparations for the
1977 Black Arts Festival*

Apollodorus, merchant-pimp who bore
The wealth of Africa to a barbarian lord,
Rolled artifice in art, a tragic flaw
Disguised to aid the statescraft in the bawd.

Not she dispensed, but took the coated pill.
Cleopatra's needle fell from hands incontinent
While Ceasar's feet stamped patterns of his will
On outspread rugs of an enchanted continent.

There was some poetry alas, Apollodorus, in
Your part, adventurer and alien, beyond
Kith loyalties, pander sublime. Nor sin
Nor history frets against the poet's bond.

Your precedent, Apollodorus is but part heeded
By new black Levantines, purse-ringed, and mortgage-beaded.

THE APOTHEOSIS OF MASTER SERGEANT DOE

Welcome, dear Master Sergeant to the fold
Your pace was firm, your passage mean and bold.

Lean your entry, in studied Saviour's form
Combat fatigued, self-styled a cleansing storm.

Let other shoulders sprout gold epaulettes
You shunned those status-greedy etiquettes,

Stayed simple Master Sergeant. The nation knew
Who was the Master; the Sergeants rendered due.

The comrade band diminished. The bloody contest played
Its grand finale. Alone the Master planner stayed

The course. The lean had rounded out. The barrack slob,
Close-crop peak-cap head affects new heartthrob

Swinger images. The tie pins are no paste.
The spoils of office, easy acquired taste

Distend the appetite, contract the scruples.
A crow may answer eagle, perched on borrowed steeples.

Flown on flags, graced by diplomatic corps
We consecrate the nightmare, kiss a nation's sore.

To mask the real, the world is turned a stage,
A rampant play of symbols masks a people's rage.

The ass that mimes the Lord's anointed wears
A face that once was human, prone to fears

But crowns are crowns. When rulers meet, their embraces
Are of presence. Absent cries make empty phrases.

The pile is high on that red carpet trail
That muffs the steps to your Inaugural Grail,

Skulls like cobbles, bones like harmattan twigs
The squeals of humans dying the death of pigs.

You missed the hisses too; a fanfare covers all.
The whine of violins at the State House Ball

Bears down the whining discords of misrule.
You've proved a grade A pupil from survivors' school.

Your worthy predecessors raise a toast
From exiled havens, or from the eternal roast

Swinging Bokassa, Macias Nguema, Idi Amin Dada
You sucked their teats, you supped from their cannibal larder,

And belched in unison. The pinnacle attained,
Next goal is duration. Shall we see you ordained

In the *Guinness Book of Records*, the Master stayer?
Youth is your ally, and appetite of a Master slayer.

Till the people's fiesta: a blood-red streamer
In Monrovian skies, a lamppost and – the swinging Redeemer.

U.S.A.

NEW YORK, U.S.A.

I.

INITIATION

Control was wrested from your pilot's hands
And yours, mid-Atlantic, hapless voyager.
Deafened by the engine's last descent
To all but disordered echoes of your feet,
Unbalanced by fake bargains, 'Duty free', you
FOLLOW THE SIGNS, WATCH FOR COLOR CODES.
Numbed by time change, low with jet fatigue,
Disgorged in tunnels tight as blindfolds,
Entrapped with lampreys rushing to their doom,
You come to a sudden stop, the world four deep
In multilingual queues.

Grim passages predict an amphitheatre
Of deadly games, of rites of menace.
A lion prowls beyond to feed these Romans' lust.
Or a minotaur? You took a time machine,
Wrong boarding pass, and here arrived in legend.
Missed your way with Christians to a pagan
Land. Its exits bleed from warning stripes
As sirens reach to clutch you by the hair.

This gash of smiles does not promote
My ease, though I trust them harmless. Native
Even to precision leers, they herd us in
On poster guards of honour, purple heart
Ablaze with instant Kodak passion. The legend?
This film star/space star/mayor/or porn queen

Toothsomely pledges: 'New York loves you!'
Forgive my innocence, does New York *know* me?
The word has turned mere gesture in N.Y.
I'll settle for a plain Visitor's Visa –
Single Entry; Exit, Multiple.

II.   LOST TRIBE

Ants disturbed by every passing tread,
The wandering tribe still scurries round
In search of lost community. Love by rote,
Care by inscription. Incantations without magic.
Straws outstretched to suck at every passing broth,
Incessant tongues pretend to a way of thought –
Where language mints are private franchise,
The coins prove counterfeit on open markets.

Hard-sell pharmacies dispense all social pills:
'Have a nice day now.' 'Touch someone.'
There's premium on the verb imperative – some
Instant fame psychologist pronounced it on TV –
He's now forgotten like tomorrow's guru,
Instant cult, disposable as paper diaper –
Firm commands denote sincerity;
The wish is wishy-washy, lacks 'contact
Positive'. The waiter barks: 'Enjoy your meal,'
Or crisper still: *'Enjoy!'* You feel you'd better!
Buses, subway, park seats push the gospel,
Slogans like tickertapes emblazon foreheads –

'Talk it over with someone – now, not later!'
'Take down fences, not mend them.'
'Give a nice smile to someone.' But, a tear-duct
Variant: 'Have you hugged your child today?'

III.   SUBWAY, NEW YORK

I too have dared (and fled) the rage
Of those primordial capsules, rape
Of motion through Manhattan's bowels,
Bronx and Brooklyn, Harlem, Queens,
Rodeo tumbrils plying shallow routes
Through Mammon's sated belly.
Hung on straphangers, shrunk
From defecation smeared as paint –
The drool of ego, fantasies unchained.
'Self-expression' belched the morning
Talk-show pundit, controversial for his pay,
'Safety valve for pent-up violence.'
He seeks to place a city's rankness
In its bowels, fool depravity
With permissive cant. I see only
Graffiti violence augmenting decibels
Of snapping strings, tuneless thought.

They are the nation's vocal chords, reels
Of buried tracks shuddering memories to life.
The clang of chain gangs – dead are they?
Forgotten? Perhaps few recognise their ghosts.
The sleek-eyed alley cat on padded feet

That pauses, darts and cleanly savages,
Prepares its feral brew of blood and loot.
Violation is native to its eyes. And fear.
Behind the ego-strut – fear. Each glance,
Resourceful as a blade, invites and stabs.

No, few recognise their ghosts.
Few recognise the time-hatched chickens
'Stomping' home to roost. With every plunge,
With every wombward rip and its unanswered
Scream, remember Bessie Smith. Remember
Muddy Waters, Leadbelly, Sojourner Truth,
Recall that other Railroad Underground,
Remember why the Lady Sang the Blues,
Remember, yes, the Scottsborough Boys,
The sweet-sad death-knell of Joe Hill,
John Brown, and oh, the much-abused,
Misunderstood, sly Uncle Tom.
I saw his patriarch face, at peace,
Reflected in a subway flash. Beside him
An old disguise, snatched at knife point,
From the museum of history's stereotypes.

IV.   THE MOST EXPENSIVE ANCHORMAN IN U.S.A.

The most expensive anchorman in U.S.A.
(A million dollars plus per annum after tax)
Hardly ever *reads* the news but, Rather
Makes a news presentation.

A sublime encounter without precedent?
The less time needed to regurgitate
The mush of instant commentary.
Abettors readily on call, by hookup
A button pushed lights up the world's
Despairing ignorance. Banality
Obeys the law of Parkinson, swells
Its reign to fill prime space and time.
The mountain heaves and groans, hems and haws,
Brings forth a Mickey Mouse: Did you note
The President was sweating when he spoke?
Would that be due to camera lights?
Or do we detect a hint of nervousness?
Could we surmise he was not giving all
The facts? Keeping something back? A hint,
A – shall we say – of more disclosures yet
To come? Of course it could be make-up.

'One moment – yes – were you about to say
His tie was knotted just a notch too tight?
He touched it once or twice I noticed. Not tugging,
Just a kind of gentle pat – now that
Could prove a gesture of significance.
I mentioned it in passing to Rick Schram.
You listening Rick? Oh, we lost the picture.
Rick? Ah, there he is. Rick, remember
That new tie of the President? It might
Become the issue, just as I predicted.'

The most expensive anchorman in U.S.A.
Rates his sneer a badge of knowing.
Armchair glib, from doughnut mix to spacecraft,
The latest launch postponement earns his scorn.

'Well, there you have it folks – one more delay.
With all the billion-dollar gadgetry,
The most advanced computerworks – it takes
A chance technician with a paper clip
To spot the ten-day glitch. Well, we hold our breath.
Is there a – *latest* forecast? The twelfth I think.
A fuel leak may be the next excuse. Or weather.
Or plumbing problems in the loo. Still
There is always chewing gum to plug a leak –
Let's hope the astronauts are listening –
You listening astronauts? Don't leave home
Without it. And now to something more dependable –
The Bhopal tragedy. With me via satellite
Is Mr. Rajiv Gandhi, Prime Minister
Of India ... Rick are you with me?'

The 'Go' was given. Post-mortem sighed, returned
To school, shed forensic laws to study
Rules of media hype. Science had bowed to gibes,
To wisecracks fuelling a nation's expectations.
The O rings lay in wait on mortal hubris ...

Mind calloused to universal loss,
Our man declined to blink, stayed squarely
On the ball. The ghoulish game began.
Reruns of fated microseconds, frame by frame
Pandered to a nation's voyeur lust. Kith and kin
The close bereaved were casual anchor fodder.
Master of Ceremonies, cool, unflappable, he
Tortures hours from moments, shakes grief loose
Of cultured silences in humane options.
The understated narrative. Taste
As sometime reticence in dread events.

Our man is jovial host to one more
'Talk show', junk food of wonder palates
In wonderland. The anchor caste rejects
Catharsis. Awe is sentiment. His newsy tongue
Licks the wound anew, bleeds raw bandages.

Rewind. Slow motion. Zoom on frame.
The expert violates the cosmos yet again
Deadsoul questions peel off, robot reel –
'There! That yellow dot. Here it comes in close-up.
Do you see the tiny prick of orange flame?'
Would that be the moment of disaster?
Do you think they knew then what was happening?
Let's have a fix on the sequence of events –
We'll turn to NASA – what do you have there, Tom?
You fellows worked out yet the schedule of disaster?
Well, an opinion then. An inspired guess?
What went on within the capsule? – I mean,
The final moments – would you like to comment?
Rather not? Rather not comment?
Now that's unheard of, rather.

The most expensive anchorman in U.S.A.
Alas, is no exception. A rival station chases
Ratings with a clone – they make a perfect
Koppel. Aliens, still your groans, their viewers
Love them. And strangers may not take their offering
Past the shrine; they'll only feed the faithless.
I plead the pangs of a space nut, self-confessed
Astronaut *manqué*; keep long liquid vigils
Launching day, East or West and nonaligned.
Agonise on every failure, celebrate

The triumphs. I'd volunteer for a voyage
But fear I'll stand accused of my profession
Which tends to the dramatic. Earthbound I remain
Vicarious stowaway on every thrust in space.

The *Challenger* will be replaced. And astronauts.
But not the most expensive anchorman in U.S.A.

v. COLUMBUS CIRCLE, N.Y.

The siren's septic saw edge sheers off
Plate-glass windows, reels off diamond flares
The sun has gouged within their tinted wombs.

A vagrant curses off the lingering fumes
Of last night's laced methyl. Trash cans
Are milestones of his quest, the inns and fields
Of leisured foraging. Contempt replies the stares.

Torsos mimic robots – daybreak, noon break, night
Break kings of dime-and-quarter sidewalks.

Sahel is cool. His wares – tan leather pouches,
Glass and coral, ivory combs and sterile *jigida*
Stake territorial claims. Slit cowrie eyes
Scan approaches for the march of law.

When it rains, the shrewd magician's sack
Transforms exotica to sleek umbrellas,
Guaranteed, in softest rain or breeze –
Auto destruct.

MUHAMMAD ALI AT THE RINGSIDE, 1985

The arena is darkened. A feast of blood
Will follow duly; the spotlights have been borrowed
For a while. These ringside prances
Merely serve to whet the appetite. Gladiators,
Clad tonight in formal mufti, customised,
Milk recognition, savour the night-off, show-off
Rites. Ill fitted in this voyeur company,
The desperate arm wrap of the tiring heart
Gives place to social hugs, the slow count
One to ten to a snappy 'Give me five!'
Toothpaste grins replace the death-mask
Rubber gumshield grimaces. Promiscuous
Peck-a-cheek supplants the maestro's peek-a-boo.

The roped arena waits; an umpire tests the floor,
Tests whiplash boundaries of the rope.
The gallants' exhibition rounds possess
These foreplay moments. Gloves in silk-white sheen
Rout lint and leather. Paco Rabanne rules the air.
A tight-arsed soubrette checks her placard smile
To sign the rounds for blood and gore.

Eased from the navel of Bitch-Mother Fame
A microphone, neck-ruffed silver filigree – as one
Who would usurp the victor's garland – stabs the air
For instant prophecies. In cosy insulation, bathed
In teleglow, distant homes have built
Their own vicarious rings – the forecast claimed
Four million viewers on the cable deal alone;
Much 'bread' was loaded on the scales

At weighing hour – till scores are settled. One
Will leave the fickle womb tonight
Smeared in combat fluids, a broken foetus.
The other, toned in fire, a dogged phoenix
Oblivious of the slow countdown of inner hurts
Will thrust his leaden fists in air
Night prince of the world of dreams.

One sits still. His silence is a dying count.
At last the lens acknowledges the tested
Hulk that dominates, even in repose
The giddy rounds of furs and diamond pins.
A brief salute – the camera is kind,
Discreetly pans, and masks the doubletalk
Of medicine men – 'Has the syndrome
But not the consequence.' Promoters, handlers
It's time to throw in the towel – Parkinson's
Polysyllables have failed to tease a rhyme
From the once nimble Louisville Lips.

The camera flees, distressed. But not before
The fire of battle flashes in those eyes
Rekindled by the moment's urge to centre stage.
He rules the night space even now, bestrides
The treacherous domain with thighs of bronze,
A dancing mural of delights. Oh Ali! Ale-e-e . . .

What music hurts the massive head tonight, Ali!
The drums, the tin cans, the guitars and *mbira* of Zaire?
Aa-lee! Aa-lee! Aa-lee *Bomaye! Bomaye!*
The Rumble in the Jungle? Beauty and the Beast?
Roll call of Bum-a-Month. The rope-a-dope?
The Thrilla in Manila? – Ah-lee! Ah-lee!

'The closest thing to death,' you said. Was that
The greatest, saddest prophecy of all? Oh, Ali!

Black tarantula whose antics hypnotise the foe!
Butterfly sideslipping death from rocket probes.
Bee whose sting, unsheathed, picks the teeth
Of the raging hippopotamus, then fans
The jaw's convergence with its flighty wings.
Needle that threads the snapping fangs
Of crocodiles, knots the tusks of elephants
On rampage. Cricket that claps and chirrups
Round the flailing horn of the rhinoceros,
Then shuffles, does a bugalloo, tap-dances on its tip.
Space that yields, then drowns the intruder
In showers of sparks – oh Ali! Ali!
Esu with faces turned to all four compass points
Astride a weather vane; they sought to trap him,
Slapped the wind each time. He brings a message –
All know the messenger, the neighbourhood is roused –

Yet no one sees his face, he waits for no reply,
Only that combination three-four calling card,
The wasp-tail legend: I've been here and gone.
Mortar that goads the pestle: Do you call that
Pounding? The yam is not yet smooth –
Pound, dope, pound! When I have eaten the yam,
I'll chew the fibre that once called itself
A pestle! Warrior who said, 'I will not fight,'
And proved a prophet's call to arms against a war.

Cassius Marcellus, Warrior, Muhammad Prophet,
Flesh is clay, all, all too brittle mould.
The bout is over. Frayed and split and autographed,

The gloves are hung up in the Hall of Fame –
Still loaded, even from that first blaze of gold
And glory. Awed multitudes will gaze,
New questers feast on these mementos
And from their shell-shocked remnants
Reinvoke the spell. But the sorcerer is gone,
The lion withdrawn to a lair of time and space
Inaccessible as the sacred lining of a crown
When kings were kings, and lords of rhyme and pace.
The enchantment is over but the spell remains.

Ile-Ife

MY TONGUE DOES NOT MARRY SLOGANS

For Odia Ofeimun

Sooner plead a writer's block, a cramp,
Akaraba worked by the envious, enchantment
Cast by a beloved siren, jealous of
That constant rival, Muse. Sooner plead
A seven-year dream of leanness, the fat to follow.
Plead a passing inhibition, overdose of reality
That stuns the mind and beggars lyric.
Blame a doctor's caveat on the brain's
Fevered contest with the world. Sooner
Lie in wait than splutter 'truths'
Decreed in metronomic swings. 'My tongue
Does not readily marry slogans,'
Said the poet. I heard it echo
In the mind's secretive dialogue with itself.
Better a wait in tense silences,
Glimpsing a promise of the future Word,
The poem unsung, the verse that kneads
Abandoned clay, and brings to pulse
The dreamt feast of all humanity.

Rats have gnawed the bloody seals
Off visionary pledges, red-rimmed boasts
Moving to the one fulfilment. Only tongues
Questioned in the field of gore dare bring
Advocacy to the sump of blood.
Yet loftiest even of these envisage future
Processes whose means do not demean the end.
The rest is cant, keen cant, the shivering child

That will not come in from cold sleet
Except the house be set ablaze for warmth.
I find no poetry in slaughter fields,
No lyric grace; redemptive passion, no.
Only that which came and went, as others –
The blaze of empires, salvation's ashes,
The crunch of cinders in time's cul-de-sac.
My tongue eschews the doctored mint
Of slogans. Dirge it may,
But not invoke the wake.

Scene:

Multi-naira clinics raised to heal.
The shelves stare empty, surgery pans are rusted.
The doctor's reassuring smile replaces
Drugs, his hand prescribes placebos,
Crosses off the hopeless case and
Saves the last pill for a worthier soul. Colonel,
Tycoon, professor, minister, all have vanished
Up the clouds. Their jet will land in Frankfurt,
London, U.S.A., where purring chariots
Waft their bodies to sequestered clinics
Far from madding crowds. These scenarios we know.

Drudge, stay-at-home physician eyes his framed
Hippocratic oath, recalls the other adage:
'Heal thyself,' and tranquillises rage.

Sooner his placebo than its slogan twin.
So, reserve my cross. Till then I will not
Dull our mutual impotence with cant,
Nor stretch the dead end of the place and time
On slogans' half tracks. Nurse,

242

The placebo that knows itself! Find
A worthier soul for that last, bitter pill.

Empty vials balloon to funeral wreaths
Kwashiorkor bellies stretch to rounded
Water pots and mimic nourishment. No,
There is no poetry yet, but sooner
Silences than tongues that tickle slogans.

Scene:

The bloated victim of a hit-and-run
Ten-day festering. After dinner motorcades
Cruise softly by, stench-proofed
By air-conditioners. Flies buzz the passersby.
A highway patrol pauses, rams oiled gears
For a rapid getaway. Crows hover, patiently.

Scene:

A child's scavenger face, pressed against
A dung heap. Its fingers are inhuman,
Claws regressed to a rooting mammal's
Probe moulting peat, rusted cans and faeces.
Onlookers keep a safety space; they think he's cursed,
Not starving.

Scene:

Police checkpoint: 'I could shoot you now,'
The lawman screams, and pulls the trigger.
An athlete's brains disperse the pleas
Of good Samaritans. Peacemakers dodge
Grey flakes on motor chassis, paste on arid tar.

You drank in splendour at the watering holes
Of academe, waxed loudly in messianic
Rounds of slogans raised as shields against
Each pleading void. Atavists of Allah
Rose and slit the throats of fellow Moslems,
Screaming, 'Mohammed was a slaving Arab.'
Ripping thighs off pepper chicken, deftly
Sliding off spiked chunks of skewered *suya*,
You dribbled slogans a thousand safety
Miles away, holding forth by Staff Club
Swimming pools: 'These *Maitatsine* only kill
The propertied, the bourgeois parasites,
Fat leeches, Mercedes-owning compradors.
Raise the toast – the revolution has begun!'
The beer foamed white – cost, college subsidised.
Midnight missed you at the barricades
But found you snoring sweetly in your mistress's
Arms, secured by campus walls, manned
Day and night by 'wage-slave proletarians'.

The ivory towers soar. Skyscrapers race
To register exclusive slogan stakes
On these disputed dunghills – Hear O Hear! –
The record is worn thin, yet the pundit's
Maledictions filter loud, rumbling drum
To surface drum of glazed wall shelters,
Rolling Maorxy-Tongue to Buddha belly:

Because the goal is one, the road is One and no other.
*The footpath shyly prying in towards the road is **not**,*
*Nor **is** a rest in meadows on the way.*
*The scent of rain, the colour of night are **not**.*

The paths of love are not, the fervour of touch is **not**.
The clasp of trembling hands on marching knees is **not**,
Nor **is** the pause to answer fear or assuage grief –
(We've censored S.O.S. from letters of the master text.)
The error of the panicked bow, once drawn, is **not**.
The horror of the self-inflicted wound is **not**.
The crumbling foothold on the precipice is **not**,
Nor is the human grasp that faltered at the edge.

Since **justice** is but One, it must
Be seized not piecemeal but entire, or not at all,
And pleas for the moment's justice shall not **be**.
No more defiant streams of spittle, no,
Not from enfeebled throats whose desperation
Douses arsonists' flames, for these are **not**.
The straw-and-wooden ramps by menaced doors,
Neighbour watched by sleepy eyes are **not**.
Grass torches flung against the threatened rape
Are **not**, nor stern exactions when the deed
Is done. For these are but illusions cast
To blur **The Goal**. The flawless Destination.
Alone it makes the one Reality. Not even faeces
Smeared on lowly walls and faces, stench
Of agents' power shall earn response
For these are mere diversions, twitches of the End,
Signposts for knowing prophets of **The Way**.
And sores are **not**, and must be left to fester.
Yaws of undernourishment gouged deeper
By neglect are **not**, for in their wells
Deepening ever with pus are glimpsed
Reflections of the distant goal, the One-Cure
Cure-for-All-Eternity of human history.

Oh lotus men, secure in your omniscient Buddha fold,
Clamant heroes of the awaited poem,
There will be random palls of restless victims,
Sprung again to life, against all foreknowledge,
Stirring in your yellowing scroll of ivory slogans.
They scream: You'll not emboss my shroud in slogans!
But if phrasemongers have indeed usurped the world,
And dreams come packaged, handy like a sausage roll,
The poet chooses: DANGER – DREAMS AT WORK.
Now mark *my* slogan well.

DRAGONFLY AT MY WINDOWPANE

So when I offer me, a medium as
The windowpane, you beat upon it
Frantic wings against unyielding tolerance?

Yet did I envy this, the unambiguous pane
And thought it clarity enough. But you must
War upon it, wings of frosted light,

And charge in thunderclaps? Each dive
Yields proof enough; your parchment shavings read:
Even clarity masks stubborn substance.

And shall this image I present not stay
Its own determined shield? Much dross
Much stone, much jewelled earth and fire

Have fed the stressing of my wall of light.
Let it content you how in me
I yield a stark view of the world, and trust

No inner warp but smudges left
By probing hands, dust of faith-flimsy wings
Distort true vision.

When darkness gathers I may dance
The world in fey reflections; or splay its truths
In a shadow play of doubts.

LOVE POTION

For a Student Believer

Still his hands embrace
Death's kingdom

Love petals from her hair
Turn ashes at the touch

Seeds in dreams alone
Burst this death's withholding

A final mockery floods
Love's winding sheet.

CAMPUS, ILE-IFE

I

When Ogun slammed his anvil down
The flinty earth of Idanre,
Its shock waves burrowed through millennia,
Surfaced in charged outcrops, sinuous
Offsprings, seven-ridged rockhills of Ile-Ife.

II

Their soil serrations read like texts
The sagehood enclave has inscribed
Upon its skin. Gnarled parasites
Retain moss-padded stranglehold
On probing shoots. For these, the sun recedes.
Nature is adept at staging mirrors
Even to the algae's slimy treachery
On rock surfaces. Their oval pools reflect
Horizons slipped askew, settling upside down.

III

The rains of July douse March embers,
Raise frail mists to shroud the grey-flecked
Blackstone of youth's stubborn being.
Cooling vapours lower in vain
On youth's foundations, ambiguous
As cotton flimsies goddesses may don
To ease the passion of fiery hills.
Graceful ageing was our prayer but,
Who can rein the restive stallion
On whose flanks the gods have chosen
To make their moist descent!

IV

Stilled are their transit squeaks.
Albino bats will probe in vain
For one familiar echo chamber, scout
Among strange frequencies. At dusk
You made this head your nest, filed
Protest flights across my roof.
Daylight found you, sagging jute bags,
Filled with mush from yet unripened fruits.
Your vampire brothers pass beneath
Sated in unholy suppers of the mind.
They cluster too for safety, but deny it.

CREMATION OF A WORMY CARYATID

Ancient caryatid, too long a host
To woodworms browsing deep within
Your charitable mass, keen mandibles
Have probed your outward piety, aired hidden
Histories through a million perforations.
The borers have worked miracles, lodged
A slow disease within your votive claims.
Their industry, invisible in my gallery gloom
Threads heartwood, hours of skilled devotion
Like spaces of the unknown creative
Hands, now a womb of dust.

Peace, peace, acquisitor heart.
Still your pangs of greed, quit longing,
Douse hunger. Shun furtive middlemen
Assailing Christian, Muslim convertites,
Ministers to aesthetic lust – 'Bring out
Your forsaken gods; this agent serves
Paymasters for apostasy.' Haggling skills
Contend. Collection rounds end in grimy
Sacks, junk bedfellow with rich rarities.
Then the salivating eye, caressing bronze
And verdigris. Fingertips read wood lore,
Spell chromatic rings that age, sublime
Patina, has glazed as inlaid traceries.
Alas, the mites have punctured hoards of lust,
Left mere form, and scooped the substance.

Wood-be telltale signs, the yellow sift
Of soft collapse alas, departed daily
On conscientious brooms, untutored dusters.

Grand personages – sages, warriors, lords,
And – the ancestor presence too? – remained
Oblivious to their second deaths. Beneath
A sky dome mimicked by a palanquin,
The royal head may hear the din of battle,
Clang of steel on shield, the roaring guns
And screams of courage, death, despair,
But not the thrust of enemies within,
Gnawing entrails of strict hierarchies:

Middle dais – lords and warriors, harem,
Diviners share vicarious power. Lower, the slave
Parade, necks halter-ornamented raw,
Strike plaintive poses on base podium,
Their place and fate among the footstool,
Mortar and pestle, knife and sacrificial rams.
Royalty engrosses all of upper level –
Beads, crown, regal whisk and treasury –
Robes cascading down to rest imperial hem
On tribute bearers, royal feet on headstool.

The ancestral plinth sheers off, obliquely,
From these mortal planes, angled thrust
In sacred isolation, an igneous outcrop
Straining at the bonds of earth.
Bird of swirling plumage, vegetal mask,
It rears at tangent, soughing skyward.
Against the mortal column a demonic lift,
Arbitrating earth and heaven, death and gods.
A ribbed cage veils the inner eye,
Its trail entwines the deeds of living –
Anvil, housepost, cock and corncob – wraps
The cyclic symmetry that ruled the carver's world.

The woodworms' evenhandedness has spared
Neither king nor beast. Lust leaks
From ramhorns, udders ooze their swell.
The fist's salute is palsied; flintlocks trickle
Dust. The stallion's heaving chest caves
Gently inward at a finger's touch.
Heartwood turned porous, time rings finely honed
To render fluid pace to ponderous limbs
Reduced to warts and acne on ancient lacquer.
O Time's aesthetic feast, enslaving eye
And mind; what futile sighs the heart exhales,
Lamenting pliant hands that shaped such heirlooms
Now succumbed to mere mortality.

The mind attunes to loss – a mercy death.
To save the grove, we isolate the tree;
Beyond all cure, uproot, incinerate.
Too ill to grace the backyard rubble, the outcast
Rides the funeral pyre. Yet, the poised hand
Briefly trembles. A passing chord in air,
Mere shard of recollection, a muted
Choral disquiet hovers, plucks at heartstrings,
Pleads a stay of execution. Healthy gods
Alas, disdain weak intercessors. Thumbs
Down-pointed urge the fate of porous caryatids,
Incite the sacrilege with match and kerosene –
Their glories, were they not of fire and sword?

The moment is richly chosen; twilight
Is favourite hour of ancestral parting. I pause
To listen. This music, when it comes
Eschews the drums of marches, trumpets, *kakaki*,
Crests home on herdsmen's flutes of reed,

Gourd xylophones, the *kora's* mournful trills
And distant echoes from dying fields
Of lords of forests, kingdoms long extinct.
Vain to search these airwaves for martial
Rings of glory, rings of anvils at the forge,
Thrust in far horizons. Only their echoes
Linger ... orphan cries, weightless grains,
Dewdrop rings entwined in spider webs,
Frail bamboo shoots. The ashes' wind sift
In abandoned hearths, grass carbon in bush fires,
Uneasy spirals snared in *gbegbe* leaves ...

    Mo ja'we gbebe
      I plucked the leaves of *gbegbe*
    Ki won ma gbagbe mi
      Lest I be forgotten
    Mo ja'we oni tete
      I plucked the leaves of *tete*
    Ki won ma te mi mo le
      Lest I be trodden under
    Ojo nlo
      The day gently passes
    Ko se wa ire
      May it serve us well
    Oju ki i mo r'oko r'oko
      The soul adapts to strange lands
    Ko gbagbe ile
      Yet ever yearns for home
    O ma mi lo ogerere
      And thus, departing, departing,
    O ma mi lo ogerere
      And thus, gently departing

The cinders of past epochs sink – but slowly.
Lack of substance clings tenaciously
To form. Pillars rise in flames of conquest,
Peel, incandescent. The reel unwinds
In timeless cycles:
A spearpoint's taper of light.
A head's defiant aureole. Shrine portals
Lower to glowing hearth, back to foundations –
Still they cling to form! Each crumbling
Motion claims new recognition. The equestrian
Loses mount but girds a viaduct's
Evanescent birth. Protean are the stallion's
Shimmering thighs. A cinder ruptures; as fanned
By hot winds, desert blown, the arches sway,
Reform as careful ruins on histories' sands.
Horsemen, groom, lance and standard
Slew half-circle, subsumed in subterranean
Fires. The field of gore glows golden,
Glory-hued to the last hurrah.

Dissolute in the dance of fire, acolytes
Abandon vestments, paraphernalia, soar
Upwards on instant flues, sink back to earth.
Kaleidoscope unflagging, a brace of peacocks
Fan new-hazed triumphal arches where
Slaves in loincloth earlier knelt in homage.
A curtain of flames is parted: glimpsed behind
Shy curtains – solemn brides, immobile gazes
Swivel on lustrous hips, their nuptial dance
Soon shrouded by the falling palanquin. Mortars
Mould superfluous hearths, their pestles
Blacksmiths' tongs for one brief, bellows' breath.

A terse tongue moves to search the ancestral train,
Finned torso of the sacred serpent. It
Finds the inner eye. The explosion
Tears all lingering shards of centre plinth,
Brings death grimaces to charred remains
Of slaves and warlords. Each head falls singly,
Each ponderous crash a shore of longing,
Refuelling the pool of ash and cinders.
It makes fine ashes. The borers worked well,
Relieved the wood of pith, left flames
An easy core to question. But – the last word
Is of water, as of the beginning;

> *Se b'omi ni o pa'na, se b'omi*
>> Is it not water that douses fire, is it not
> *Ni o pa'na. Se b'omi . . . ?*
>> Water that douses fire? Is it not water?

Rain comes as arbiter, *deus ex machina*
Dark horse flexing hooves on roofs of zinc,
Dives to earth, scuffs telltale ashes,
Draws a curtain of discretion on the altar hearth.
This sudden coyness to forestall a second,
Third or fourth idolatry? Urn fetish?
Relic sales? Display of wooden tibia,
Mildly charred, authenticated. Scoops
Of ash in pouches of *egungun* clothing.
Remnant speartip. Halter chip. A cowrie,
Slit intact . . . The intercessor gone,
May mortals not recoup the loss that borers made?

Alas, what's gone is gone. The rain affirms the loss.
Grace that was a fiery dying congeals.
The skies have opened, gods and hero-gods
Blot all traces of their erstwhile dance
With mortals, uphold the lore of pinpricks
Mere woodworms may pronounce on golden realms.
A pottage of ash and cinders marks the spot,
A loathsome mound, pocked by drum throbs
Pressing from the skies. . . . Yes, these stubborn
Sceptres, exorcised, yet marrying earth to heaven!